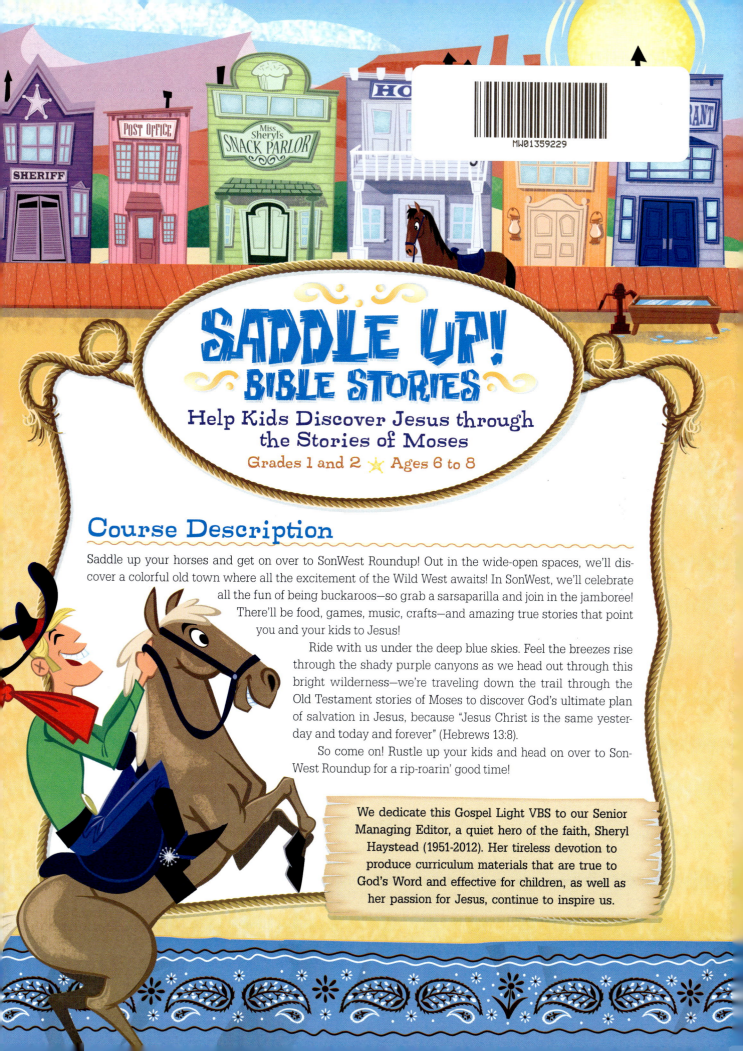

SADDLE UP! BIBLE STORIES

Help Kids Discover Jesus through the Stories of Moses

Grades 1 and 2 ★ Ages 6 to 8

Course Description

Saddle up your horses and get on over to SonWest Roundup! Out in the wide-open spaces, we'll discover a colorful old town where all the excitement of the Wild West awaits! In SonWest, we'll celebrate all the fun of being buckaroos—so grab a sarsaparilla and join in the jamboree! There'll be food, games, music, crafts—and amazing true stories that point you and your kids to Jesus!

Ride with us under the deep blue skies. Feel the breezes rise through the shady purple canyons as we head out through this bright wilderness—we're traveling down the trail through the Old Testament stories of Moses to discover God's ultimate plan of salvation in Jesus, because "Jesus Christ is the same yesterday and today and forever" (Hebrews 13:8).

So come on! Rustle up your kids and head on over to SonWest Roundup for a rip-roarin' good time!

We dedicate this Gospel Light VBS to our Senior Managing Editor, a quiet hero of the faith, Sheryl Haystead (1951-2012). Her tireless devotion to produce curriculum materials that are true to God's Word and effective for children, as well as her passion for Jesus, continue to inspire us.

TABLE OF CONTENTS

Teaching Helps
Leading a Child to Christ .... inside front cover
Course Description 1
Course Overview 3
Decorating Your Center 4
Effective Teaching Tips 5
Bible Story Center Basics 6

Sessions
Session 1 • Born to Save 8
Session 2 • Promise of Power 14
Session 3 • Passover Rescue 20
Session 4 • Perfect Provision 26
Session 5 • Law of Love 32

Bible Story Skits 38

Evangelism Opportunity
This symbol highlights portions of the lessons that provide special opportunities to explain the gospel message to children. Look for this symbol in the Tell the Story section of each lesson.

Make the theme come alive for your VBS children! As leaders of the Bible Story Center, take on new names inspired by a western town: Horseshoe Sue, Mesquite Pete, Cowboy Cal, etc. Dress according to the theme in western clothing, cowboy boots, jeans, western shirts, suede vests, etc. Decorate your room as described on page 4 and play songs from the *Music & More CD*. You'll have as much fun as the kids—maybe more!

Gospel Light VBS
Jesus Every Day

Publishing Director, Donna Lucas • **Senior Managing Editor,** Sheryl Haystead • **Associate Managing Editor,** Karen McGraw • **Senior Editor,** Mary Gross Davis • **Editorial Team,** Anne Borghetti, Kristina Fucci, Janis Halverson • **Contributing Editors,** Deni Hardgrave, Laurie Head, Sherri Martin, Judy Nyren • **Production Manager,** Peter Germann • **Art Director,** Lori Hamilton Redding

Founder, Dr. Henrietta Mears • **Publisher,** William T. Greig • **Senior Consulting Publisher,** Dr. Elmer L. Towns
Editorial Director, Biblical and Theological Content, Dr. Gary S. Greig

© Gospel Light. It is illegal to photocopy or reproduce this material in any form.

COURSE OVERVIEW

Bible Theme: Hebrews 13:8

Ultimate Points	Bible Story	Jesus Connection	Bible Verse
1 Ultimate PLAN	**Born to Save** Exodus 1:1–2:10	God cared about the Israelites and sent Moses to help them. God sent Jesus because He cares about me!	"For God so loved the world that he gave his one and only Son, that whoever believes in him shall not perish but have eternal life." John 3:16
2 Ultimate POWER	**Promise of Power** Exodus 3:1–4:31	God used His power to help Moses. Jesus' power is big enough to help me— no matter what!	"In this world you will have trouble. But take heart! I have overcome the world." John 16:33
3 Ultimate RESCUE	**Passover Rescue** Exodus 5:1–12:51	God saved the Israelites from slavery in Egypt. Jesus' death and resurrection can save me from sin and give me eternal life!	"I am the resurrection and the life. He who believes in me will live, even though he dies." John 11:25
4 Ultimate TRUST	**Perfect Provision** Exodus 16:1–17:7	The Israelites could trust God to provide for them. I can trust Jesus to take care of me every day!	"I am the bread of life. He who comes to me will never go hungry." John 6:35
5 Ultimate LOVE	**Law of Love** Exodus 19:1–20:21; 24:12; 25:10-22	God gave commands for the Israelites to follow. Jesus' new command is to follow Him and love others!	"A new command I give you: Love one another. As I have loved you, so you must love one another." John 13:34

DECORATING YOUR CENTER

A few simple decorations can transform an ordinary classroom into the Golden Saddle Theater. Use a variety of real items and/or painted backdrops. *Wild West Décor & More* contains patterns and more detailed instructions. For additional information, see the decorating segment of the *Overview DVD*. Also, check out myvbsparty.com and the Gospel Light VBS Facebook page for more decorating tips and ideas from VBS directors all over the world!

The Golden Saddle Theater

Create an old-timey Western theater where dramatic stories of Bible adventures fascinate kids of all ages!

Level 1

★ Use these easy decorating supplies, available from Gospel Light. Attach **Decorating Posters, Bible Teaching Posters, Preprinted Wall Murals** and **Wall Cutouts** to the walls. Add color with **Pennants** and **Attendance Chart**.

★ Designate an area for your stage. Arrange **chairs** for your audience facing the stage. Enlarge and trace the **Golden Saddle Theater Sign** onto butcher paper or cardboard, paint and cut out. Attach to the wall above your stage or hang it from the ceiling.

Level 2

★ Set a **box marked "PROPS"** and/or an **antique trunk** on your stage to hold **Bible Story Props** for each day. Look into *Saddle Up! Bible Stories* for five daily sidebars that each contain great decorating and prop ideas to bring Bible stories to life!

★ Find a **large wooden picture frame** to fit the Bible Story Posters. Paint frame on both sides with **gold spray paint**. Insert the Bible Story Poster for the day in the frame. Make a sign that reads "Now Playing" and attach to frame. Set frame on a stand or **artist's easel** to display. You'll need a second set of Bible story posters to use both sides of the posters as directed in *Saddle Up! Bible Stories*.

Level 3

All the patterns references below are available in Wild West Décor & More.

★ Enlarge and trace **Theater Stage Backdrop Pattern**. Paint and attach on wall for stage area.

★ Enlarge and trace **Theater Box Seat Pattern** onto butcher paper. Paint, cut out and attach to a side wall.

★ Enlarge and trace **Gaslight Sconce Pattern** onto butcher paper, creating several gaslight sconces. Paint, cut out and attach to side walls.

★ Enlarge and trace **Gas Lamp** and **Chandelier Patterns** onto cardstock or cardboard. Paint, cut out and hang from the ceiling.

EFFECTIVE TEACHING TIPS

Preparation Is the Key

★ Pray for God to prepare the hearts of your children—and yours, as well! Use the questions provided in the Daily Recap to carefully consider everything that took place during each session of VBS so that you will be better prepared for the next!

★ Be prepared before each day begins. Have all materials ready for use so that you can focus your attention on the children, not on what you may have forgotten!

★ Read through the entire lesson several times so that you know the lesson well.

★ Know the Ultimate Point and Jesus Connection lesson focus for each day. Repeat these words often to connect each activity to the session's Bible story and verse.

★ Practice telling the story, selecting storytelling options that will keep kids actively engaged in learning.

Conversation Is an Art

★ In addition to telling the Bible story, be prepared to make good use of informal conversation before and after the story. Suggestions are provided for each lesson to help you focus these moments toward the Goals for Each Child.

★ Review the conversation suggestions provided. Think of ways you might tailor or build on these ideas to meet the needs of the children in your class. Write down any other ideas or questions you might ask, and keep them with you during the lesson. Listening to children's responses to your open-ended questions will help you discover what they know (or don't know) about a particular topic.

★ Plan to listen as much as you talk. Look directly at the child who is talking. Demonstrate your interest by responding to the specific ideas the child expressed.

★ Know each child's name and use it in positive, loving, affirming ways throughout the lesson. Look for opportunities to express praise and encouragement.

★ Be sensitive to each child's home situation and plan your conversation to include the variety of family situations represented in your class and among their friends.

★ Stay with your children as they complete activities. Whenever possible, sit at children's eye level. They need to know that you are there, ready to help and ready to listen.

★ Most importantly, pray for God to guide all your discussions with the children placed in your care.

★ If you have a child acting disruptively, move near the child as you speak. Asking the child to answer a question can also help get him or her back on track.

Bible Story Center Basics

You play a very important part in VBS, whether you are the leader in the Bible Story Center or a helper. Each day as you prepare, read the Heart Prep to get your heart and mind ready to lead children to the Bible truths for that session. Then study the Goals for Each Child. Knowing these goals for each child helps you know what learning will be taking place during the lesson. Study the Bible story Conclusion; this conversation gives you a natural opportunity to talk with children about joining God's family.

The Bible Story Center is divided into two simple parts to help children learn important Bible truths: Tell the Story and Apply the Story.

Tell the Story (15-20 minutes)

Through each Bible story, kids will discover Jesus in the stories of Moses. Display Bible story posters from the *Bible Teaching Poster Pack* for children to see while listening to the story. (The Bible story posters are also available on the *Rip-Roarin' Assemblies DVD*.)

Telling the story in small groups is ideal, both for building relationships and allowing opportunity for interaction. But the story can also be told effectively to a large group—just make sure the storyteller is well-prepared and animated. Seat additional helpers among children to guide children's behavior.

Story Starter

Introduce the Bible story with a quick and fun activity to help children connect everyday life with the Bible lesson they are about to hear. Then give Bibles to children to use during the story. Begin each story with a brief prayer.

Bible Story

Each Bible story is written in language appropriate for third- to fourth-grade children. (Note: If you are teaching a mixed age-level group, the version found in this *Saddle Up! Bible Stories* is appropriate for both younger and older children.) During the story, volunteers read brief Scripture passages or answer quick involvement questions. This helps keep kids actively involved in the story.

Bring the Bible Story to Life!

Use these quick and easy decorating suggestions to create awesome settings for your story. And since kids don't just listen to a story—they LIVE it, keep interest levels high by using the creative suggestions for involving children in the telling of the story. Even if you're new to storytelling, these ideas can help you become a seasoned pro.

Conclusion

After the main story, summarize the Bible truths for the children. Relate the lesson to what children are learning about Jesus. Each story conclusion also offers an opportunity for evangelism.

Drama Option: Instead of telling the Bible story, have a team of volunteers come to each Bible Story Center and perform the Bible Story Skits found on pages 38-48 of this book. Older children may enjoy performing the skits themselves.

Prayer

Each story ends with a silent and/or group prayer. Praying with your children helps them see the relevance of prayer in whatever they do.

Apply the Story (10-15 minutes)

Lead children in applying the lesson to their lives through discussion and activities in the *Mount 'Em Up* student guide. (Note: An Active Review game is suggested as an option for each session. This game leads kids to talk about the Bible story in an active way.) Whether or not you choose to tell the Bible story in a small or large group, these life-application activities are best suited to be used by small groups that facilitate discussion. This time includes:

★ Bible story review

★ Bible verse discussion

★ Application activity and discussion

Head 'Em Up! student guides

These colorful and fun pages not only bring the theme to life, but are also must-have keepsakes of your children's adventures at SonWest Roundup! Get a copy of each *Head 'Em Up!* student guide and look through it to familiarize yourself with its contents. Included is a fun family activity children can take home and do with their families.

Wild West Quest

Each session's *Head 'Em Out!* includes a fun family activity. Part of the activity involves drawing a picture or taking a photograph. Challenge your children to bring in the drawing or photograph to the next session of SonWest Roundup to receive a small prize. Display the drawings and photographs in your classroom.

SESSION 1 ★ GRADES 1 & 2
BORN TO SAVE

Bible Story
Exodus 1:1—2:10

Bible Verse
JESUS SAID For God so loved the world that he gave his one and only Son, that whoever believes in him shall not perish but have eternal life. John 3:16

Jesus Connection
God cared about the Israelites and sent Moses to help them. God sent Jesus because He cares about me!

Goals for Each Child
1. PARTICIPATE in a story about how God loved His people when they were in trouble and sent Moses to help them;
2. DISCUSS ways God shows He loves us, and why He sent Jesus to help us;
3. THANK God for sending Jesus to show His love for me;
4. CHOOSE to join God's family as the Holy Spirit leads.

Daily Animal—Armadillo
Armadillos have poor eyesight. Because they are easily startled and frightened, they're often run over by cars. They need to be delivered from danger! Just as the Israelites needed God to deliver them from danger, we all need Jesus to deliver us from sin!

Teaching Tip
Information about each Daily Animal is included here so that you can talk to kids about the ways the animal reinforces the Jesus Connection for each session.

Heart Prep

Welcome to SonWest Round-up VBS! This week we'll have a blast as we ride, rope and explore in a Wild West town! In our Bible lessons, we'll follow Moses as God used him to lead the Israelites out of slavery in Egypt.

Imagine what it must have been like to pack up everything and head into the unknown: the Promised Land held great promise, but also unseen risks and hostile tribes. (That sounds a lot like what people faced heading into the Wild West!) We'll discover how much even we modern-day cowpokes are like the Israelites and how God's unchanging truths connect to our lives today!

In this first session, kids will be introduced to the Israelites, a family God had chosen for His very own. God had promised to bring salvation and blessing to all people through them. And yet, when we meet them, they are slaves to the Egyptians, victims of their circumstances and powerless to help themselves. But God heard their cries. He cared about their need and showed Himself faithful by sending Moses!

Just as God cared about the Israelites and sent Moses to help them, so God sent Jesus to all of us. We are slaves, too—slaves to sin and powerless to help ourselves. But God's Ultimate Plan has been in motion since before time began! Because He cares about each of us, He sent Jesus to rescue us from the slavery we are in and the punishment we deserve. God's love for us is so great that He gave up His own Son to free all who believe in Jesus from sin's slavery!

This week gives you the exciting chance to help kids discover how Moses and the Israelites show us a picture of Jesus and all people. Pray that kids would come to understand how digging into God's Word reveals Jesus in God's plan for redemption from Genesis to Revelation. It's the Ultimate Plan—from the Ultimate Savior, who is the same yesterday, today and forever!

Daily Recap

At the end of each lesson, take time to reflect on what happened. Use these questions as a guide:

* What worked well today? What nugget of truth did you discover from God's Word?
* As you prepare for Session 2, ask God to help you keep focused on Jesus during the busy VBS schedule.
* Read aloud the name of each child in your group. Pray for each one, inviting God to help that child understand His love and salvation this week.

Materials

For more story props, see page 10!

* Bibles
* *Music & More CD* and player
* Session 1 Bible Story Posters A and B from *Bible Teaching Poster Pack* or *Rip-Roarin' DVD*
* Session 1 *Head 'Em Out!* student guides
* gift-wrapped box or gift bag
* old trunk or box labeled "PROPS"
* soft ball or beanbag
* ballpoint pens

Optional—

* gift box or bag holding a small prize or individually wrapped candy for each child

TELL THE STORY
(15-20 minutes)

Preparation: Display Session 1 Bible Story Poster A. Place a bookmark at Exodus 1 in your Bible and refer to it as you tell the story.

Place gift-wrapped box or gift bag in a trunk or prop box.

Story Starter

Howdy! Welcome! I'm (Pecos Pete), the storyteller here at the Golden Saddle Theater. Get ready for a boot-stompin' good time—and an amazing true story from the Bible!

But before we get to the story, I want to show you this. Remove gift-wrapped box or gift bag from trunk. **What's this? Yep! A gift. Now I need three volunteers.** Volunteers stand beside you. **Let's pretend I give (Ali) this gift.** Pretend to give gift. **But then I tell (Ali), "Pay me five dollars for this." Is that really a gift? Why?** Volunteers respond.

Let's pretend I give (Toby) this gift. Pretend to give gift. **Then I tell (Toby), "I want this back tomorrow." Is that really a gift? Why?** Volunteers respond.

Now what if I give (Tiffany) the gift? Pretend to give gift. **But (Tiffany) says, "I don't WANT your gift." Is that really a gift? Why?** Volunteers respond. **What does she have to do for this to be a GIFT?** Volunteers respond. Give gift to child, asking child to hold gift during the story. (Optional—Tell children that there are gifts inside for everyone to receive at the end of story time.)

Yep! Today, we're talking about gifts. When do we give gifts? Volunteers respond. **Yes, birthdays! Christmas! When babies are born! That reminds me of a story about a baby. This baby WAS a gift! He was a gift to God's people—and his name was Moses.**

Born to Save

Exodus 1:1—2:10

A Family Grows

Long, long before our story begins, there was a man named Joseph. He was taken AWAY from his home, to the land of Egypt. Joseph helped the king of Egypt, called Pharaoh, to save the Egyptians from starving. So Pharaoh really LIKED Joseph. He even asked Joseph's family to come to Egypt to live! Since Joseph had ELEVEN brothers who had lots of kids, a BIG family came to Egypt!

Years and YEARS went by. Joseph's family grew larger. And LARGER! This BIG family was God's people, the Israelites. And the family kept on GROWING. It grew for the next four hundred years!

Now, FOUR HUNDRED years later, a new Pharaoh was in charge of Egypt. He saw that there were many, MANY Israelites—and he started to worry. He asked, "What if all these people join my enemies and go to WAR against me? I've got to STOP them." That's when Pharaoh came up with Evil Plan Number ONE. **Show one finger.**

"I'll make those Israelites my SLAVES!" the Pharaoh said. "They will work hard for ME in the hot sun! They'll make bricks and build cities for me. THAT will get rid of some of them!" **Show brick.**

And suddenly, the Israelites were SLAVES. Strong men used whips to make them work very hard. **Play "Whip"**

Bring the Bible Story to Life!

Lay blue tarp, bedspread, etc. on the floor for the Nile River. Place one or more potted plants along the edge of the "river."

In your trunk or box, place props to display at key moments in the story: brick, baby doll and blanket, basket. If you cannot find objects, bring in pictures printed from the Internet.

Large Group Tip

If you use pictures, project them onto large screens in your Bible Story Center so all can see them.

Small Group Tip

Give objects or pictures to volunteers to show at appropriate moments.

At the times indicated, play the sound effects available on the *Music & More CD*. Lead children to act out the suggested actions as you tell the story.

> **Skit Option**
> A fun alternative or supplement to this or any Bible story is to ask teachers, youth helpers or other volunteers to perform the "Ultimate Plan" Bible Story skit on pages 39-40.

sound effect from CD. Pharaoh THOUGHT that this hard work would get RID of some Israelites, but no. MORE Israelites were born every day!

An Evil Law

So Pharaoh came up with Evil Plan Number Two. **Show two fingers.** He sent for the women who helped Israelite mothers when they were having babies. **Show baby doll wrapped in a blanket.** Pharaoh told these women to KILL any baby boy that was born! But the women protected the baby boys instead.

Then Pharaoh came up with Evil Plan Number Three. **Show three fingers.** This plan was even WORSE! Pharaoh said, "Every Israelite boy baby must be thrown into the NILE RIVER!" **Play "Splash" sound effect from CD.**

Imagine how you'd feel if your family was expecting a baby! But ONE Israelite family didn't have to imagine. A baby boy was born to them and they LOVED him! The baby's mother hid him for three months. **Play "Crying Baby" sound effect from CD.** It must have been HARD to hide a wiggling, giggling, squirming, crying, baby boy!

But one day the mother knew she couldn't keep the baby hidden much longer. So she made a plan—but it WASN'T an Evil Plan. It was a GOOD plan! **Show basket.** She got a basket and covered it with tar to make it waterproof. When the basket was ready, she gently laid her baby boy in it. **Lay doll in basket.** She covered him up well. **Tuck blanket around doll.** Then she and her daughter Miriam took the basket down to the Nile River.

The mother set the waterproof basket in the tall reeds at the edge of the water. Miriam stayed behind, hiding in the reeds to keep an eye on her baby brother. Miriam's mom left, probably wondering, *What will happen to my baby?*

A Princess' Help

Soon, Miriam heard voices. **Show Session 1 Bible Story Poster A.** Then, Miriam saw where the voices had come from—it was Pharaoh's DAUGHTER and her MAIDS! She probably scrunched down lower so they wouldn't see her. **Scrunch down.** The princess and her maids had come to the river to bathe. Uh-oh! Pharaoh wanted to KILL Israelite baby boys. What would his DAUGHTER do to an Israelite baby boy?

Before Miriam knew it, the princess saw the basket. She told her maid, "Bring me that basket!"

The maid brought the basket to the princess and the princess opened it. WHAT? Yes! It was a baby. **Play "Crying Baby" sound effect from CD.** He was crying. And the princess DIDN'T throw him into the water. She DIDN'T toss him to a crocodile! She said, "He's an Israelite baby! Don't cry, baby." She turned to her maids. "He must be hungry. Get someone to FEED him!"

Miriam could see that the princess wasn't going to hurt her baby brother. So she ran to the princess. She said, "I know a woman who can feed the baby for you! Should I get her?"

"Yes! Go get her NOW." Miriam must have run ALL the way back to her house and back again—with her MOM! When they got back to the princess, the princess handed the baby to his own MOTHER. **Cradle baby in arms.** "Here," the princess said, "Feed this baby. Take care of him until he is older. I will PAY you."

So Miriam's mother took her own baby home again! What a gift! The family got to care for him until he was old enough to live with the princess in the palace. And the princess named the baby "Moses."

But even though Moses was safe, God's people were still in trouble. They were still SLAVES. As Moses grew to be a

man, life for the Israelites got HARDER. They prayed and prayed, asking God to free them from slavery. God heard their prayers. He had a plan to set them free—and guess who was part of that plan? Moses! This baby would grow to be the VERY person God was going to send to help His people and get them out of slavery!

Conclusion

God's people were in trouble. But God had a plan to help them. God protected Moses when he was little so that Moses could grow up and lead God's people out of slavery. Moses was God's GIFT to the Israelites!

Show Session 1 Bible Story Poster B. **This story of Moses is important because it points us to God's Ultimate Plan. Like the Israelites, we're slaves, too! The Bible tells us that we are all slaves to sin (Romans 6:16). Sin is what we think, do or say that disobeys God. But God had His Ultimate Plan. He gave Moses to save the Israelites from slavery. And God gave Jesus to save us from sin!**

Our Bible verse for today is John 3:16. Jesus said, "For God so loved the world that he gave his one and only Son, that whoever believes in him shall not perish but have eternal life." When we believe in Jesus and ask God to forgive our sin, we can join God's family.

Sending Jesus was the main part of God's Ultimate Plan! Each day at VBS, we're going to talk about other ULTIMATE things God gives us as part of His family.

When we join God's family, we become part of God's Ultimate Plan! (Invite children interested in knowing more about becoming members of God's family to talk with you or another teacher after class. See "Leading a Child to Christ" on the inside back cover.)

Prayer

Let's name some ways God shows He loves us. Volunteers tell. Pray aloud briefly, thanking God for those specific ways and for the greatest way He showed His love—by the gift of His Son, Jesus.

APPLY THE STORY
(10-15 minutes)

Bible Story Review

To review the Bible story, lead children to complete the "Help in Trouble!" activity in *Head 'Em Out!* As children work, ask the questions below to guide conversation.

★ **Why did Pharaoh want to hurt Israelite babies?** (He was afraid that there were too many Israelites. He was afraid they would fight against him.)

★ **How did God help Moses' family to protect Moses?** (God brought the princess. She found Moses. She didn't hurt him. God helped Miriam speak to the princess and bring her mother. Her mother was paid to take care of her own baby!)

★ **The Israelites were slaves to Pharaoh. Why do you think the Bible says we are slaves to sin?** (We can't

Active Review

Children sit in a circle to play Hot Potato. Play songs from *Music & More CD*. As music plays, children pass brick around the circle. After a few moments, stop the music. The child holding the brick answers, or chooses a volunteer to answer, one of the questions above. Repeat until all questions are answered or as time permits.

get rid of the wrong things we do. We need Jesus to forgive us.)

⭐ **Why did God make His Ultimate Plan to send Jesus?** (God loves us. God doesn't want us to be slaves to sin. God wants us to be part of His family.)

Moses and Jesus were born HUNDREDS of years apart. Show Old Testament portion of Bible. **Moses was born way back in Old Testament times. Jesus was born in New Testament times.** Show New Testament portion of Bible. **But both babies were God's GIFTS. Both came to rescue people who were in trouble! The things that happened to Moses help us to know more about Jesus.**

Jesus died to take the punishment for our sins so we can be forgiven. Jesus' death and resurrection made the way for us to join God's family. Joining God's family is a gift. It is free; we don't have to pay for it. We never have to give it back. If we receive this gift, we are part of God's family forever!

Life Application

Today's verse is John 3:16. Many people say it's their favorite verse in the Bible! Read John 3:16 aloud with children from Bible or *Head 'Em Out!* **What does this verse say about God?** Volunteers respond. **Remember the gifts? God LOVES us. That's why He GAVE us His own Son, Jesus! Jesus took the punishment for our sin. Jesus made the way for us to be forgiven and become part of God's family.**

Children complete the "It's a Gift!" activity in *Head 'Em Out!* Ask questions such as:

⭐ **What are some things you know about Jesus?** (Jesus is God's Son. Jesus loves us. Jesus died to take the punishment for our sins. Jesus rose again and is alive. Jesus forgives our sins when we ask Him.)

⭐ **Why is it important for all people to know that God sent Jesus?** (Every person is a slave to sin. Everyone needs to know that Jesus can forgive us.)

⭐ **How do we receive God's gift of Jesus?** (Agree with God that we are slaves to sin. Believe that Jesus died and rose again so we could be forgiven. Ask Jesus to forgive us. Ask to join God's family.)

What is today's Ultimate Point? Pause for children to respond, "Ultimate Plan!" **All week we're going to learn more about the ULTIMATE things God gives the members of His family. God gave Jesus because He loves us. Jesus is the most important part of God's Ultimate Plan!**

Ultimate Connection Signs

For each session, display the appropriate Ultimate Connection Sign. Flip from one side to the other for a handy visual aid to your conversaion with children about the Ultimate Points and Jesus Connections each day.

God cared about the Israelites and sent Moses to help them. God sent Jesus because He cares about me!

SESSION 2 ★ GRADES 1 & 2

PROMISE of POWER

Bible Story
Exodus 3:1—4:31

Bible Verse
JESUS SAID *In this world you will have trouble. But take heart! I have overcome the world.* John 16:33

Jesus Connection
God used His power to help Moses. Jesus' power is big enough to help me—no matter what!

Goals for Each Child
1. PARTICIPATE in a story about how God showed His power to help Moses;
2. DISCUSS ways to depend on Jesus' power to help us;
3. THANK Jesus for His power to help me;
4. CHOOSE to join God's family as the Holy Spirit leads.

Daily Animal—Lizards
Lizards are cold-blooded. That means they have to get warm to be able to move around with any speed. Only after it soaks up the sun's power can a lizard get warm enough to move freely. Just as lizards need the sun for the power to move, so we need God's power—given to us by Jesus!

Heart Prep

Entering the workforce after being a stay-at-home mom for 22 years, I felt inadequate and ill-prepared. I really thought the people who hired me would soon discover that they had made a giant mistake. How could I be an editor?

Moses had a similar reaction when God called him to lead His people out of slavery. How could he, a fugitive and murderer, be a spokesman for God? (Makes being a stay-at-home mom look pretty good!) Besides that, he wasn't a very good "upfront guy!" Moses wasn't equipped to do the job. That is what makes Moses' story so great! It wasn't Moses who freed God's people from Egypt—it was God. God showed Moses His power through a burning bush and the shepherd's staff Moses carried. God revealed His power through a bush and a stick!

As we discover the power of Jesus through this story about Moses, remember the astounding yet simple things Jesus said and did that proved He is God's Son. Spitting in the dirt, He used the mud to cover a blind man's eyes—and the man could see (John 9)! A woman was healed by merely touching the hem of His garment (Mark 5:25-34). His words brought a dead man back to life (John 11:1-45). His power is greater than any obstacle or opportunity we face!

When we obediently put one foot in front of the other and trust in God to work through us, we see Him do amazing things. I love my job and am so blessed to be part of your life as you lead kids at VBS. So, even if you feel inadequate and ill-prepared to introduce children to Jesus today, remember that Jesus is the One doing this. He has the power you need. You don't have to depend on your own resources. Rest in His Ultimate Power and watch what He does! (And don't forget to tell us your stories at myvbsparty.com or on our Facebook page. We're inspired to hear what Jesus is doing through you!)

Daily Recap

At the end of each lesson, take time to reflect on what happened. Use these questions as a guide:

★ What was your greatest struggle today? How did Jesus reveal His power in the midst of your struggle? How did you respond?

★ Thank God for His power! Invite Him to prepare the hearts of the kids to respond to their need for Jesus.

★ Be prepared to briefly tell about the time when you became a member of God's family.

Materials

★ Bibles
★ *Music & More CD* and player
★ Session 2 Bible Story Posters A and B from *Bible Teaching Poster Pack* or *Rip-Roarin' DVD*
★ Session 2 *Head 'Em Out!* student guides
★ objects or pictures that represent fears (toy spider, toy shark, toy snake, photo of a storm, etc.)
★ toy microphone
★ trunk or prop box
★ soft ball or beanbag
★ ballpoint pens

For more story props, see page 16!

Tell the Story

(15-20 minutes)

Preparation: Display Session 2 Bible Story Poster A. Place a bookmark at Exodus 3 in your Bible. Refer to it as you tell the story.

Place objects or pictures and toy microphone in trunk or prop box.

Story Starter

Welcome back! I had a great time talking with you yesterday about God's Ultimate Plan and His great gift—Jesus! We're going to learn more about Moses and Jesus today. What do you think is in my trunk today? Volunteers guess.

Remove (toy spider). **Yikes!** Toss (spider). **That was a spider! I'm afraid of spiders. Are any of you afraid of spiders? I'm kind of scared to find out what else is in here!** Continue to remove items. (You need not toss each one—but you can!) Discuss the fear each item represents.

Remove and show microphone. **Why would someone be afraid of a microphone? Yes! People are often afraid to speak to a lot of people. Did you know MOSES was afraid to speak to a lot of people? He was! And that is JUST what God asked him to do. Show me your pointer fingers. We're going to use them in the story!**

Bring the Bible Story to Life!

Place brown fabric (burlap, tablecloth, sheet, etc.) on ground to mimic the desert floor. Place a potted plant with tissue-paper "flames" on it at one end of the fabric.

In your trunk or box, place props to display at key moments in the story: walking stick, stuffed sheep, toy snake. If you cannot find objects, bring in pictures printed from the Internet.

At the times indicated, play the sound effects available on the *Music & More CD*. Lead children to act out the suggested actions as you tell the story.

Promise of Power

Exodus 3:1—4:31

A Burning Bush

It had been many years since Pharaoh's daughter found baby Moses. Now Moses was a grown man—in fact, he was an OLD man! And he wasn't living in Pharaoh's palace. He was living in the desert, leading and caring for sheep. **Show walking stick and stuffed sheep; walk in place.**

One day, Moses led the sheep near a big mountain. Suddenly, Moses saw something very strange. **Play "Burning Bush" sound effect from CD.** Moses walked nearer. In front of him, a bush was on FIRE—but the bush didn't burn up! **Point at potted plant.** The flames just kept burning and burning. How could this BE?

Moses was so surprised! He said, "What's going on? This is amazing! Why doesn't the bush burn UP?"

Suddenly, Moses heard a VOICE. **Point at ear.** The voice was coming from the burning bush—and it was saying HIS NAME!

"Moses! Moses!" Moses knew the voice must be GOD's voice!

Moses answered, "Yes? I'm right here!" **Point to self. Show Session 2 Bible Story Poster A.** "Don't come any closer," God said. "Take off your sandals. You're standing on holy ground." So Moses quickly took off his sandals. **Remove shoes.**

Then God said, "I am the God of your father, the God of Abraham, the God of Isaac, the God of Jacob." Moses hid his face, afraid to look at GOD!

God said, "I've seen how sad My people are. I've heard their prayers. I am going to help them! I am going to bring them out of Egypt to a beautiful land, full of wonderful things. And Moses! I am sending YOU to lead them!" **Point outward.**

A Stuttering Man

Moses was surprised! He stammered, "But . . . I'm NOBODY." **Point to self.** "What makes You think I can lead the Israelites out of Egypt?"

"I will be WITH you!" God said. "And to PROVE that I am with you, I tell you this: When you have brought My people out of Egypt, you will all worship Me right here—at this mountain."

Moses didn't think anyone would believe him! Moses asked, "What if I go to the Israelites and say, 'God sent me to you' and they ask, 'God WHO? What is His name?' What do I say THEN?"

Point upward. God said, "I AM WHO I AM. Tell the Israelites, 'I AM is His name.' Now GO! Bring the Israelite leaders together. Tell them I sent you to lead them into the land I have promised to give them. They will listen to you. Then go to Pharaoh and tell him to let the people GO." **Point away.**

God continued, "Pharaoh won't WANT to let his slaves go. So I will have to make him change his mind."

Moses whined, "The people won't listen to ME." **Point to self.** "They'll say, 'God appeared to HIM? HA!'"

So God said to Moses, "What's that in your hand?" **Show walking stick.** It was Moses' walking stick.

God told Moses, "Throw it on the ground." Moses threw it down and the stick turned into a SNAKE! **Show toy snake. Play "Hissing Snake" sound effect from CD.** Yikes! Moses jumped back as far as he could! **Jump back.**

But God said to Moses, "Now reach out and grab the snake by the tail." Moses must have been terrified! But he reached out and grabbed the snake—and as soon as he did, it became a STICK again. **Show walking stick.**

"When the Israelites see you do THAT, they will believe that I appeared to you, and that I am God." **Point upward.**

Then God said, "Put your hand inside your clothes." Moses put his hand inside his clothes. When he took it out again, his hand was covered with a DISEASE. It was all white and crusty. Ugh! **Point at hand and look scared.**

God said, "Put your hand back inside your clothes." Moses did. When he took his hand out again, it was healthy! **Point at hand and smile.**

"If you show the people these amazing miracles and they STILL don't listen, take water from the Nile River. Pour it out onto the ground. **Point at ground.** The water will turn to BLOOD!"

Moses whined, "But God . . . please . . . I'm SLOW. I don't talk very well." **Point at mouth.**

God asked Moses, "I WILL be with you, Moses—and with your mouth! I'll TELL you what to say. Get going!" **Point away.**

But Moses just didn't want to DO this. So he pleaded with God, "PLEASE! Send somebody ELSE!"

God was NOT happy with Moses! But God is very kind. He said, "Your brother Aaron speaks well. He is on his way to you right now. You can tell HIM what to say. **Point outward.** Aaron can talk to the people. You can use your staff to do the amazing things I gave you the power to do."

When Aaron arrived, Moses told him about God's message and the amazing things God had helped Moses to do. Aaron was excited. He and Moses rounded up all the Israelite leaders. Aaron told them everything that God had told Moses. Moses showed God's power through the amazing miracles God said to do—and the people DID believe.

> ### Skit Option
> Teachers, youth helpers or other volunteers perform "A Leader for God?" on pages 41-42.

The Israelites were so glad! God cared about them! **Point up.** He knew they were slaves. He was going to HELP them! The people bowed down and worshiped God. They thanked Him for His power and love. **Point up with both hands.**

Conclusion

Moses was SCARED to do the job God asked him to do! But God promised to help him. He SHOWED Moses His power. God promised Moses He would help him every step of the way.

Show Session 2 Bible Story Poster B. This story of Moses points us to another Ultimate Point—Ultimate Power! You see, there will be times when we're scared, too. We can be scared that we're not good enough or smart enough to do something God wants US to do. But just as God promised to give Moses the power to speak to Pharaoh and to lead the Israelites, God promises Jesus' Ultimate Power to us.

Our Bible verse today came from Jesus Himself. In John 16:33 He says, "In this world you will have trouble. But take heart! I have overcome the world." Jesus has ULTIMATE POWER! And He promises that if we are members of His family, we can always ask Him for His power and help—and He'll give it to us!

To have Jesus' Ultimate Power to help us every day, we must first become members of God's family! (Invite children interested in knowing more about becoming members of God's family to talk with you or another teacher after class. See "Leading a Child to Christ" on the inside back cover.)

Prayer

Invite volunteers to complete this sentence prayer: **Dear Jesus, I am glad You have Ultimate Power to help me . . . .** End the prayer time by thanking Jesus for His love and power.

APPLY THE STORY
(10-15 minutes)

Bible Story Review

To review the Bible story, lead children to complete the "Where's the Power?" activity in *Head 'Em Out!* As children work, ask the questions below to guide conversation.

- **Why was Moses afraid?** (God wanted him to talk to the Israelites. God wanted him tell Pharaoh what to do. God wanted him to lead the Israelites out of Egypt.)

- **How did God show Moses that he could depend on God's power?** (Turned his stick into a snake, then made it a stick again. Made his hand white with disease. Healed his hand.)

- **After Moses had seen God's amazing miracles, what did he say?** (I'm scared. Send someone else to do the job.)

- **How else did God help Moses do this job?** (Promised to be with him. Told Moses his brother Aaron could do the talking.)

Active Review

Children stand in a group. A volunteer stands in front of the group, facing away from them. Volunteer tosses soft ball or beanbag over shoulder toward group. The child who catches the ball or beanbag answers, or chooses a volunteer to answer, one of the questions above. Repeat, using other volunteers, as time allows.

God may never ask us to do a job as big as the one He gave Moses. But God WILL ask us to do things. And He promises to give us POWER to do those things, just like He gave Moses. When we join God's family, God gives us this Ultimate Power—Jesus' power!

Life Application

Read John 16:33 aloud with children from Bible or *Head 'Em Out!* **These are Jesus' words. What does Jesus say we will have?** (Trouble.) **EVERYONE has trouble! Bad things happen to EVERYONE. There will be times when we feel sad, scared or unhappy. But Jesus can give us Ultimate Power. His power helps us not to worry or be scared. It makes us strong when we think about doing wrong. Jesus will give us power to do what is right!**

Have children complete the "Power Words!" activity in *Head 'Em Out!* Ask questions such as:

- **Jesus says He has overcome the world. What does that mean?** (Jesus is stronger than anything that happens. Jesus' power can help us in any situation.)
- **How does it make you feel to know that Jesus is stronger than anything?** (Glad Jesus is strong! Brave when I'm scared. Thankful that Jesus can help me when something is hard to do.)
- **Why do we need Jesus' power?** (We are not very strong on our own. So we don't have to worry. We can trust Jesus instead.)
- **What can we do when we feel worried, scared, angry or upset?** (Read the Bible. Remember Jesus can help. Sing songs that remind us about Jesus' power. Pray and ask Jesus for His power and help.)

What is today's Ultimate Point? Pause for children to respond, "Ultimate Power!" **Jesus gives His power to every member of God's family. We can always ask for His power and help, no matter what. Having Jesus' power doesn't mean we're going to be able to lift elephants over our heads! It means that when we feel scared or helpless, we can know that Jesus will help us! We can remember that Jesus is powerful. We can ask Him for His power. Then, we can trust Him to help us—and not worry!**

SESSION 3 ★ GRADES 1 & 2

PASSOVER RESCUE

Bible Story
Exodus 5:1—12:51

Bible Verse
Jesus Said: I am the resurrection and the life. He who believes in me will live, even though he dies. John 11:25

Jesus Connection
God rescued the Israelites from slavery in Egypt. Jesus' death and resurrection can rescue me from sin and give me eternal life!

Goals for Each Child

1. PARTICIPATE in a story about how God rescued His people from Egypt at Passover;

2. DISCUSS why we all need for Jesus to rescue us and what it means to believe in Jesus;

3. THANK Jesus for dying on the cross and rising to life again so that I can join God's family;

4. CHOOSE to join God's family as the Holy Spirit leads.

Daily Animal—Horse

A cowboy or cowgirl's best friend is their horse. Once your horse knows the way home, it can take you there, even when you are lost or confused. We all need Jesus to rescue us from slavery to sin and take us home as members of God's family. Jesus knows the way home!

Heart Prep

When my two sons were both under the age of four, they wandered out the (locked and dead-bolted) front door and got lost in our busy beach neighborhood. I was terrified! I frantically searched the street in front and the alley in back. There was no sign of them! My heart was sick. I wanted to lie down and die. I dialed 9-1-1 and cried out, "I've lost my boys!" The calm voice on the other end of the phone told me not to panic—she knew where my boys were!

When I had gathered my boys safely back home, I prayerfully pondered what the Lord was trying to teach me. God gave me a glimpse of His heart for the lost that day. His heart aches for a world full of children who are lost and don't know their way home to Him. He made the way through Jesus. He gives us the opportunity to show the way to the lost ones He loves!

Today's lesson connects to God's great plan of redemption for all people. The Passover was and is a vivid picture of the heart of God's plan—Jesus' sacrificial death to take the punishment that we deserve for our sin.

God's instructions to the Israelites were clear: Each man was to select a perfect one-year-old male lamb for his family. The man was to slaughter the lamb and put the lamb's blood on the doorframe of his house so that death would pass over the house and God's wrath on the Egyptians—the death of all firstborn sons, animal or human—would not harm them.

John calls Jesus "the Lamb of God who takes away the sin of the world" (John 1:29). Jesus is God's perfect Lamb to be sacrificed. His blood was shed on the wooden cross so that He could receive God's wrath against sin on our behalf. He has protected us from what we deserve. Instead of death, we receive eternal life—because Jesus is the resurrection and the life!

As you study the Bible story and the Bible verse today, ask God to help you explain how the story of Passover reminds us how much God loves us—so much that He sent Jesus to take the punishment for our sins and provide for our Ultimate Rescue!

Daily Recap

At the end of each lesson, take time to reflect on what happened. Use these questions as a guide:

★ What was difficult for the kids to understand about this story? What about this lesson amazed the kids? What grossed them out or scared them?

★ Which children seemed most interested in talking about joining God's family? Which ones still seem to have questions? Ask God to give you the opportunity and the words to talk further with these children.

★ Thank God for His relentless pursuit of each child at your church's VBS. This may have been the first time some were told what Jesus did for them!

Materials

For more story props, see page 22!

★ Bibles

★ Session 3 Bible Story Posters A and B from *Bible Teaching Poster Pack* or *Rip-Roarin' DVD*

★ *Music & More CD* and player

★ Session 3 *Head 'Em Out!* student guides

★ marker

★ 5 paper plates

★ trunk

★ soft ball or beanbag

★ ballpoint pens

 TELL THE STORY
(15-20 minutes)

Preparation: Display Session 3 Bible Story Poster A. Place a bookmark at Exodus 5 in your Bible. Refer to it as you tell the story.

Use a marker to draw each of these expressions on a separate paper plate: happy, sad, surprised, afraid, angry. Place paper plate masks in trunk or box.

Story Starter

I'm so glad to see you here at the Golden Saddle Theater again today! It's been so much fun getting to know each of you. I've got something in my trunk to show you, but first I'll need five volunteers to help me. Choose five volunteers, remove paper plate masks from trunk and distribute them.

One at a time, ask volunteers to hold the masks over their faces. As each mask is shown, invite remaining kids to imitate each expression. Invite volunteers to tell, or choose a volunteer to tell, how a person with that expression might feel.

Point to the mask with the surprised expression. **Today we're going to hear about some SURPRISING things.** Point to the mask with the sad expression. **We're also going to hear about some SAD things.** Point to the mask with the fearful expression. **We'll hear about things that made some people very AFRAID.** Point to the mask with the angry expression. **And things that made Pharaoh ANGRY.** Point to the mask with the happy expression. **But all these things finally made Moses and God's people very HAPPY!**

Thank volunteers and ask them to pass masks to five others, who will stand at the front and hold their masks over their faces whenever they think the feelings described are reflected by their mask's expression. Other children imitate the expression.

Passover Rescue

Exodus 5:1—12:51

Let My People Go

Moses and Aaron went to Pharaoh and told him, "God has sent us. God says to let His people go!" But Pharaoh wasn't scared of God! "WHY should someone as important and powerful as ME listen to this God of yours? I don't know this God you're talking about! And I'm NOT going to let my SLAVES go!" **Cross arms, shake head no.**

Moses and Aaron asked AGAIN. Pharaoh said NO—and decided to make things HARDER. **Show brick.** Pharaoh said that the Israelites had to find the straw to make bricks but still had to make the same number of bricks! The

Bring the Bible Story to Life!

Cut a doorframe from brown butcher paper or some brown paper bags. Tape to a wall. (Optional: At the appropriate time in the story, use a paintbrush to brush red paint on the paper doorframe.)

In your trunk, place props to pull out and display at key moments in the story: brick, toy snake, fly swatter, bandages (for boils), ping-pong balls (for hail), paintbrush, matzo bread. If you cannot find objects, bring in pictures printed from the Internet.

At the times indicated, play the sound effects available on the *Music & More CD*. Lead children to act out the suggested actions as you tell the story.

Israelites were working harder than EVER. And they were MAD at Moses!

Moses asked God, "Why did You ever send me? Things are worse than before!"

God told Moses, "I've heard my people's prayers. Tell them I WILL rescue them from slavery. I AM God." And God sent Moses and Aaron back to Pharaoh AGAIN.

But Pharaoh still didn't care what God said. Even though Aaron threw down his walking stick and God turned it into a snake, Pharaoh wasn't impressed. **Show toy snake.** But Pharaoh's magicians did tricks with snakes, too. So it was time for God to show that HE has Ultimate Power! So God sent plagues.

> **Skit Option**
> Teachers, youth helpers or other volunteers perform "Great Wise Man?" on pages 43-44.

Terrible, Awful, Really Bad Things

Plagues are terrible, awful, really bad things. **Kids repeat, "Terrible, awful, really bad things" every time you say the phrase.** And the first terrible, awful, really bad thing was turning the water in the Nile River to BLOOD. Yuck! AND all the fish in the river died. What a stinky MESS! But Pharaoh still said, "NO!" He would not let the Israelites go. **Cross arms; shake head no.**

So the next terrible, awful, really bad thing happened. This time, God sent MILLIONS of frogs! **Play "Frogs" sound effect from CD.** Leaping and croaking and jumping—frogs were ALL OVER!

Pharaoh called for Moses. "I'll let your people GO if you'll just get RID of the frogs!" Moses prayed. The frogs all died! But then, Pharaoh broke his promise! **Cross arms; shake head no.** "The Israelites are NOT going!" he stormed.

So it was time for the next terrible, awful, really bad thing. It was gnats—tiny, buzzing, flying in everyone's eyes, nose and mouth. **Play "Gnats" sound effect on CD.** Gnats were EVERYWHERE! It was terrible! Still Pharaoh said, "NO! The Israelites CANNOT go!" **Cross arms; shake head no.**

The next terrible, awful, really bad thing was flies—tickling, buzzing, biting flies—crawling and flying on everyone and everything. **Swat with fly swatter.** But Pharaoh still wouldn't let the Israelites go. **Cross arms; shake head no.**

Since having BUGS everywhere wasn't terrible, awful, and really bad ENOUGH, now all of the herds of animals belonging to the Egyptians got SICK. **Play "Livestock" sound effect on CD.** Hundreds and THOUSANDS of cows, horses, camels, donkeys, sheep, goats—were sick or dying or dead! But the Israelite animals were healthy and well! Still, Pharaoh refused to obey God. **Cross arms; shake head no.**

The next terrible, awful, really bad thing was that the people and animals of Egypt developed painful sores on their bodies. **Show bandages.** But no Israelite had a single sore! Even so, Pharaoh REFUSED to obey God! **Cross arms; shake head no.**

Then another terrible, awful, really bad thing came. It was a HAILSTORM. Ice rained down from the sky! **Toss ping-pong balls.** The hail beat down on the plants and knocked fruit and leaves off of trees. Most of the food was RUINED. But where the Israelites lived, NO hail fell at all! STILL, Pharaoh refused to obey God. **Cross arms; shake head no.**

The next terrible, awful, really bad thing was locusts—bugs like grasshoppers. **Play "Locusts" sound effect on CD.** They were EVERYWHERE. And they ate EVERY plant left alive. But Pharaoh was stubborn. "NO!" he shouted. **Cross arms; shake head no.**

Then another terrible, awful, really bad thing happened. God sent DARKNESS. **Lower or turn off lights.** There was no sun or moon for three days. But it was LIGHT where the Israelites lived! Still, Pharaoh refused to obey God! **Cross arms; shake head no.**

The Passover

Finally God told Moses there would be one last terrible, awful, REALLY bad thing. Moses warned Pharaoh, "At midnight, all the firstborn sons in Egypt—animal or human—will die. Warn Pharaoh."

Show Session 3 Bible Story Poster A. God also told Moses how to keep the Israelite families safe. Moses told everyone God's instructions: "Put the blood of a perfect male lamb on the tops and sides of your doorframes. Then the plague of death will 'pass over' your houses." **Show paintbrush; pretend to paint doorway.**

Moses also told the people to prepare and eat a special meal. Each family was to eat the meat of the lamb whose blood was used on their doorframe. They were to eat bitter herbs to remind them of the bitterness of slavery. **Show matzo bread.** They ate bread made without yeast to remind them of how quickly they were going to leave Egypt. God called this the Passover meal. They were to eat this same meal every year to help them remember how God freed them from slavery. Even today, people do this to remember how God freed the Israelites.

God's people followed all the instructions to protect their families. How sad that Pharaoh STILL refused to obey

God—even when Moses warned him this would happen! At midnight, every firstborn male Egyptian—even animals—died. But every Israelite boy was safe!

In the middle of the night, Pharaoh called Moses to the palace. "Get your people—and GO!" Pharaoh cried. FINALLY! Pharaoh let the Israelites go.

The Israelite slaves were all ready. Hundreds and THOUSANDS of them came out of their houses and began to follow Moses. **Walk in place.** They were leaving Egypt FOREVER! No more would they be slaves. God had set them free!

Conclusion

The Israelites were FREE! They were not slaves! God rescued them out of Egypt and out of slavery. Show Session 3 Bible Story Poster B. This story of Moses points us to God's Ultimate Rescue—Salvation in Jesus. "Salvation" means to be rescued or protected. God made a way for the Israelites to be rescued from the last plague.

The Bible says Jesus is the Lamb of God (John 1:29). The Israelites were rescued by putting lamb's blood on their doorframes. Jesus let His blood be spilled on a wooden cross. Jesus willingly died to take the punishment for our sins so that we can join God's family. He died—but Jesus didn't stay dead! Three days later, Jesus came back to life and is alive today!

Salvation in Jesus is the Ultimate Rescue! It is a gift given to anyone who believes in Him. (Invite children interested in knowing more about becoming members of God's family to talk with you or another teacher after class. See "Leading a Child to Christ" on the inside back cover.)

Prayer

Let's tell Jesus how thankful we are that He loves us and made it possible for us to join His family. Lead children in repeating prayer after you, one phrase at a time. **Thank You, Jesus, for loving us. Thank You for taking the punishment for our sins. We are glad that You are alive! Thank You for making the way for us to join Your family. In Your name, amen.**

APPLY THE STORY
(10-15 minutes)

Bible Story Review

To review the Bible story, lead children to complete the "Alike or Different?" activity in *Head 'Em Out!* As children work, ask the questions below to guide conversation.

- **Name a plague God sent on Egypt.** (Water became blood. Frogs. Gnats. Flies. Animals died. Boils. Hail. Locusts. Darkness. Death.)

- **What did the Israelite people do at the Passover?** (Painted lamb's blood on their doorframes. Ate a special meal.)

Active Review

Children line up and take turns tossing a soft ball or beanbag into a trashcan. Whenever a toss lands in the trashcan, child answers, or chooses a volunteer to answer, one of the questions above. Repeat as time allows.

⭐ **How does the lamb's blood remind us of Jesus?** (Jesus is the Lamb of God. Jesus let His blood be spilled on a wooden cross.)

⭐ **Why does everyone need Ultimate Rescue—salvation that comes from Jesus?** (Everyone sins. Jesus took the punishment for sins. Jesus made the only way to become part of God's family.)

God loved the Israelites. He made a way for them to be freed from slavery. We are also slaves—to sin! But Jesus made a way for us to be rescued! Ultimate Rescue is being saved by Jesus. It means we can be forgiven for our sins, be part of God's family and live with Jesus forever!

Life Application

Read John 11:25 aloud with children from Bible or *Head 'Em Out!* **What does this verse say we will do if we believe in Jesus?** (We will live, even though we die.) **That sounds really strange. But it means that if we are part of God's family, even though our bodies will die someday, we will live forever with Jesus in heaven. That's what Jesus means when He says He is "the resurrection and the life." "Resurrection" means to be alive again after dying. Jesus will make His family alive again with Him in heaven!**

Have children complete "Believe It!" activity in *Head 'Em Out!* Then ask questions such as:

⭐ **What are some things you know about Jesus?** (Jesus is God's Son. Jesus loves us, gives us power. Jesus died so that we can join God's family.)

⭐ **What are some things you'd like to know about Jesus?** Children respond. **How can you find out these things?** (Read the Bible. Ask parents or teachers. Go to church. Listen to stories about Jesus. Pray to Jesus.)

What is today's Ultimate Point? Pause for children to respond, "Ultimate Rescue!" **Ultimate Rescue by Jesus begins with three things. First, we agree that we are sinners. Second, we believe that Jesus died to take the punishment for our sin. Third, we choose to ask Him to forgive our sins and make us part of God's family. When we join God's family, we get to know Jesus more every day. Then we can learn to be like Him in what we do and say.**

SESSION 4 ★ GRADES 1 & 2
PERFECT PROVISION

Bible Story
Exodus 16:1—17:7

Bible Verse
JESUS SAID *I am the bread of life. He who comes to me will never go hungry.* John 6:35

Jesus Connection
The Israelites could trust God to provide for them. I can trust Jesus to take care of me every day.

Goals for Each Child
1. PARTICIPATE in a story about how God's people learned to trust Him to provide for their needs;
2. DISCUSS reasons we can trust in Jesus to take care of us;
3. THANK Jesus for His always giving me exactly what is best;
4. CHOOSE to join God's family as the Holy Spirit leads.

Daily Animal—Cow
Cows provide people with dairy products every single day. Giving us animals that provide food reminds us of the ways Jesus provides the things we need.

Ultimate TRUST

Heart Prep

Imagine what the Israelites must have thought when they woke up to see manna on the ground. They all said, "What is it?" (*Manna* means, "What is it?") Manna was God's perfect provision for the Israelites. Even though they didn't know what it was, it was JUST what they needed! By providing His people with manna, God showed that He loved them and that they could trust Him every day for everything. God provided bread from Heaven for the Israelites and He provides Jesus, the Bread of Life, for us. Like the Israelites, we need to trust in Jesus' salvation, grace and ability to provide what we need.

My oldest son and his wife will soon graduate from college; they have no job, no place to live—and are expecting their first child. As I try not to panic about how their needs will be met, I'm excited to see them trust God to provide perfectly! In moments of uncertainty and fear, they keep turning to God who sought and saved them.

In what ways do you struggle with worry? Maybe you know where your next meal is coming from but you are concerned about being a good example to the kids at VBS. How do you look to Jesus to meet your daily needs? Second Peter 1:3 tells us, "His divine power has given us everything we need for life and godliness though our knowledge of him who called us by his own glory and goodness." We can trust Jesus to meet our needs daily—physically and spiritually—as we live for Him. The Bread of Life calls us to come to Him. He promises to satisfy our souls and meet our needs now and forever!

Daily Recap

At the end of each lesson, take time to reflect on what happened. Use these questions as a guide:

★ Think back to today's session: What physical, spiritual and emotional needs did you notice for the kids in your care? How did you see Jesus meet those needs?

★ What worked well today? Pray for the energy to finish VBS strong.

★ As you prepare for the final session of VBS, pray for each child by name. Ask God to water the seeds that were planted this week.

Materials

For more story props, see page 28!

★ Bibles
★ Session 4 Bible Story Posters A and B from *Bible Teaching Poster Pack* or *Rip-Roarin' DVD*
★ *Music & More CD* and player
★ Session 4 *Head 'Em Out!* student guides
★ marker
★ index cards
★ white snack food (oyster crackers, popcorn, etc.)
★ resealable snack-sized plastic bags
★ rubber bands
★ trunk
★ soft ball or beanbag
★ ballpoint pens

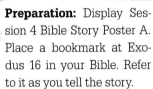

Tell the Story
(15-20 minutes)

Preparation: Display Session 4 Bible Story Poster A. Place a bookmark at Exodus 16 in your Bible. Refer to it as you tell the story.

Write "FREE" on separate index cards, preparing one "FREE" card for every three or four children plus one to use an an example. Hide cards around room.

For each child, seal a portion of the snack food in a bag. Secure sets of three to six sealed bags with rubber bands. Set bags in trunk or box.

Large Group Option

If you are telling the story in a large group, place several "FREE" cards under seats in your storytelling room. Children who find a "FREE" card pass snacks to others.

Story Starter

Hey, everyone! Welcome back to the Golden Saddle Theater. Today, we're looking for something like this. Show a "FREE" card. **There are some "FREE" cards hidden around the room. If you find one, bring it to me and you'll get something FREE! I'll give you a snack for yourself and several of your friends.** Give each child who brings a "FREE" card a set of snack bags for themselves and several others. **In today's story we're going to hear about the FREE food God gave His people!**

Bring the Bible Story to Life!

Place brown fabric (burlap, tablecloth, sheet, etc.) on ground to mimic the desert floor. On the fabric, place several clay jars or bowls that look like they may be from Bible times.

In your trunk, place some or all of the following props to show as directed in the story: crackers, honey, lidded dish containing gummi worms, walking stick, bottle of water. If you cannot find objects, bring in pictures printed from the Internet.

At the times indicated, play the sound effects available on the *Music & More CD*. Lead children to act out the suggested actions as you tell the story.

Perfect Provision

Exodus 16:1—17:7

Desert Complaints

After leaving Egypt, Moses led the Israelites to the land God had promised to give them! They were so excited! Moms and dads, kids, grandmas and grandpas, all walked with bouncing steps. They were not slaves any more! **March in place.**

But they walked day after day and week after week. They got farther from Egypt and their sad lives of slavery. After a couple of months of walking, the people had lost the bounce in their step. **March slower.** This was HARD! And they started COMPLAINING. "Are we THERE yet? When will we GET to this Promised Land? I'm HUNGRY!" **Hold hand over stomach.**

They even forgot how BAD life was in Egypt! They complained, "In Egypt, we had meat every day—and all the bread we could eat! Why didn't God just let us die there?" Soon, they were ANGRY. They said to Moses and Aaron, "You've brought us out here just to STARVE to death!"

Of course, God heard them. And of COURSE, God knew JUST what to do! He told Moses to tell the people, "In the evening, you will have meat to eat. Then, BREAD will rain bread down from the SKIES. Go out and gather it each day. On the sixth day, gather twice as much."

Miraculous Provision

So Moses and Aaron told the Israelites, "Today you will see AGAIN that God has HEARD your complaints. He will give you meat to eat in the evenings and bread in the morning. You won't be hungry! You THINK you've been complaining about US— but you've been complaining about GOD!"

Play "Quail" sound effect from CD. That evening, THOUSANDS of quail flew toward the camp, so low to the ground that the people could easily catch them. The birds were EVERYWHERE! So there was plenty of quail meat for everyone to eat.

Then, the next morning, there on the ground was a fine flaky . . . SOMETHING! It looked like frost on the ground. The Israelites looked at it and asked each other, "What is it?" **Scratch head.** No one had a clue what it was!

Show Session 4 Bible Story Poster A. Moses said, "THIS is the bread God has given you to eat. God said to gather enough for everyone in your tent." The Israelites immediately started gathering the bread. They called it *manna,* which means, "What is it?" It tasted like crackers with honey. **Show crackers and honey.** Moses told them, "Don't save ANY of it. Eat it all or throw it away."

But not EVERYONE listened to Moses. Maybe some people thought God might not send manna again! So they tried to save some. **Place crackers in dish and replace lid.** But when they went to get it for breakfast, it was full of worms and smelled bad. **Remove lid and pull out gummi worms.** Moses was upset! These people were NOT trusting God to give them what they needed!

But God loved His people. And He kept on giving them what they needed—every day. Every morning He sent them manna. They gathered what they needed each morning. Every sixth day, Moses told them, "Gather twice as much manna. Whatever you plan to cook, do it today. God has said that tomorrow is a day of rest. So set aside the leftovers for tomorrow." When they did JUST what God said, the manna was fine the next morning. It didn't smell bad and there were no worms in it!

Every single day for FORTY YEARS, God sent His people manna. **Count forty on fingers by tens.** He proved that He loved His people and was taking care of them! God even had Moses put some manna in a jar to keep so that the people would ALWAYS remember that they could trust God to take care of them!

Rock Water

The Israelites kept on walking through the hot, dry desert toward the Promised Land. **March in place.** Now they were traveling through a place where there wasn't ANY water to drink. **What do you think the Israelites did?** Yes! They whined to Moses, "Give us water to drink!"

But Moses said, "Why are you pestering me? And more than THAT, why are you doubting God? Don't you trust Him YET?"

But the thirsty people couldn't think about ANYTHING else. They complained even more! "Why did you drag us out here to the desert—to die of THIRST?" they wailed.

Moses was so upset! He prayed to God, asking, "What can I DO with these people? Any minute now they will kill me!"

God knew what the people needed. And God told Moses exactly what to do. "Go on ahead of the people. Take some of the leaders with you. Bring your walking stick." **Show walking stick.** This was the same stick Moses had used to show God's power to Pharaoh.

God gave more instructions. Moses listened. Then, he did just what God said. While the leaders were right there watching him, Moses lifted his walking stick high. He swung it HARD against a large rock. **Swing walking stick.** When the stick hit the rock, the rock cracked WIDE open—and WATER poured out! **Play "Rushing Water" sound effect from CD.** There was enough water for EVERYONE, people and animals alike! **Show a bottle of water.**

God ALWAYS provided for His people as they traveled. Every day, God gave them the food and water they needed—right up until the time when they moved into the land He had promised them!

Conclusion

God loved His people and provided what they needed every day! Even when the people forgot God's kindness, even when they complained, God proved they could trust Him to care for them.

Show Session 4 Bible Story Poster B. This story shows us another Ultimate Point—Ultimate Trust. This picture shows a time when Jesus had just fed a huge group of people. He gave them miraculous FREE food, like God had given manna to the Israelites. In John 6:35, Jesus said to these people, "I am the bread of life. He who comes to me will never go hungry." When we join God's family, we can trust Jesus to take care of us like God took care of the Israelites. But Jesus came to

Skit Option

Teachers, youth helpers or other volunteers perform "You Gave Us WHAT?" on pages 45-46.

give us something more. He came to give us God's love and help us join God's family. As part of God's family, we can trust Jesus to take care of our bodies. But more than that, He will meet our need for God's love, too.

 Do you want Ultimate Trust? You can trust in Jesus! When we are part of God's family, we can trust Jesus will meet our needs in the very best way. (Invite children interested in knowing more about becoming members of God's family to talk with you or another teacher after class. See "Leading a Child to Christ" on the inside back cover.)

Prayer

Invite children to share situations in which they or people they know need God's help and provision. Lead children in prayer, mentioning the situations and people mentioned. End the prayer time by thanking Jesus that we can always trust Him to give us what we need.

APPLY THE STORY
(10-15 minutes)

Bible Story Review

To review the Bible story, lead children to complete the "Every Single Day!" activity in *Head 'Em Out!* As children work, ask the questions below to guide conversation.

★ **Why were the Israelites unhappy and complaining?** (They were hungry, thirsty. They forgot how bad life in Egypt was. They thought they were better off in Egypt. They were mad at God and Moses.)

★ **What did God do to provide food for them?** (Sent quail for meat. Sent manna to eat every morning.)

★ **How did God provide the Israelites with water?** (Moses hit a rock in the desert and water came pouring out.)

★ **What things can we trust Jesus to provide for us?** (Forgiveness for our sins. Power when we are scared. The way for us to join God's family. Help to have what we need.)

God was with the Israelites. He heard all their complaints. And He gave them what they needed. Today, we can have Ultimate Trust that Jesus knows what WE need, too. Jesus knows better than we do what's best for us! We can trust in Him to provide exactly what's best for us, each and every day.

Active Review

A volunteer closes eyes while you hide a soft ball or beanbag in the room. Volunteer looks for ball or beanbag as remaining players say "hot" or "cold" to indicate whether volunteer is near or far from item. When item is found, volunteer answers, or chooses another child to answer, one of the questions above. Repeat as time allows.

Life Application

Read John 6:35 aloud with children from Bible or *Head 'Em Out!* **Jesus doesn't mean that when we trust in Him we will never feel hungry or thirsty. He means that He will give us the thing we need MOST! What do you think we need most?** (God's love. To belong to God's family. Salvation in Jesus.) **Jesus DOES give us food to eat, water to drink, homes to live in and people to take care of us. But when He calls Himself the "Bread of Life," Jesus means that He gives us even MORE than what our bodies need. We can trust Jesus to give us the things we need most—like God's love and salvation—every day!**

Have children complete the "Why Trust Jesus?" activity in *Head 'Em Out!* Ask questions such as:

- **What are some things you know about Jesus?** (Jesus is God's Son. Jesus loves us. Jesus died so that we can be forgiven for our sins.)

- **What would you tell a friend who asks why you trust Jesus to take care of you?**

- **What is something you want to trust Jesus to help you with today?** Ask children to think about this question for a moment. Volunteers who wish to do so may share their answers. End with a few moments of silent prayer.

What is today's Ultimate Point? Pause for children to respond, "Ultimate Trust!" **We all need different things every day. Knowing that we can trust Jesus to be with us, to love us and help us is amazing! Jesus is One we can trust. He is the very BEST Person to help us, no matter what we need!**

SESSION 5 ★ GRADES 1 & 2
LAW OF LOVE

Bible Story
Exodus 19:1—20:21; 24:12; 25:10-22

Bible Verse
JESUS SAID A new command I give you: Love one another. As I have loved you, so you must love one another. John 13:34

Jesus Connection
God gave commands for the Israelites to follow. Jesus' new command is to follow Him and love others!

Goals for Each Child
1. PARTICIPATE in a story about how God's people learned to follow God's commands;
2. DISCUSS Jesus' great love and describe ways we can obey His new command to love others;
3. THANK Jesus for helping me love others like He loves me;
4. CHOOSE to join God's family as the Holy Spirit leads.

Daily Animal—Prairie Dog
Prairie dogs live together in colonies, caring for each other and warning each other of danger. In the same way that prairie dogs accept each other and care for each other, Jesus wants us to accept, love and care for the other members of our colony—God's family.

Heart Prep

Rules, rules, rules! When it comes to rules are you more of a "rule breaker" or a "rule maker"? I am probably a little of both, depending on my situation and mood. I am so glad that God is not wishy-washy like me! The Ten Commandments God gave Moses and the Israelites were given to protect them spiritually, physically and relationally! God's rules are always in our best interest—because He loves us!

Even though God's commands were given for the people's well-being, they still didn't obey them. None of us perfectly obeys them! Because of that, we need the Savior. That's why God sent His very own Son. Jesus obeyed those commands perfectly and died on a cross so that we can be forgiven for our sins and become members of God's family. As members of God's family, His Holy Spirit helps us to live out the truth of the Ten Commandments. And through the Holy Spirit, we can obey Christ's commands to love God with all our heart, mind, soul and strength, and to love others, too!

At this last session of VBS, sing a little louder. Do the motions a little bigger (you know you want to!). Let your love for Jesus shine and cause you to look for more ways to show His love so that kids will experience Jesus in unforgettable ways!

Daily Recap

At the end of each lesson, take time to reflect on what happened. Use these questions as a guide:

★ What was the best thing you learned this week? What was the best thing you think the kids learned this week?

★ Thank God for the things that happened this week—the best, the worst and the most laughable! Ask Him to help you plan ways to stay in contact with the kids you taught.

★ Ask the Holy Spirit to help you and your children understand and hold onto all of the wonderful things you discovered during SonWest Roundup VBS.

Materials

For more story props, see page 34!

★ Bibles

★ Session 5 Bible Story Posters A and B from *Bible Teaching Poster Pack* or *Rip-Roarin' DVD*

★ *Music & More CD* and player

★ Session 5 *Head 'Em Out!* student guides

★ several instruction books (computer book, cookbook, appliance manual, etc.)

★ trunk

★ soft ball or beanbag

★ ballpoint pens

TELL THE STORY
(15-20 minutes)

Preparation: Display Session 5 Bible Story Poster A. Place a bookmark at Exodus 19 and refer to it as you tell the story. Place books in trunk.

Story Starter

Today is our last day at the Golden Saddle Theater. It's been great getting to know you this week. I'm going to miss seeing you every day—so be sure to come back on Sundays! We'll have a great time!

  Let's see what's in my trunk one last time! Show instruction books, one at a time. Read titles aloud. **What kind of book is this? What does it help us do?** Volunteers respond. When all books are shown ask, **How are these books alike?** (They help people learn to do something.)

  These books all help us learn how to do things. Show Bible. **But today we're going to talk about THIS book. The Bible helps us learn the MOST important things EVER! Get your fingers ready for this story. They will be busy while we hear how God taught His people some important things!**

Bring the Bible Story to Life!

On a wall, post a tall mountain cut out from brown or black butcher paper. In the story, when directed to walk fingers up- or downward, walk fingers up or down the paper mountain. Tape caution tape to the bottom of the mountain.

In your trunk, place some or all of the following props to show as directed in the story: walking stick, soap, bowl, washcloth, length of caution tape, large lightning bolt cut from white or yellow paper. If you cannot find objects, bring in pictures printed from the Internet.

At the times indicated, play the sound effects available on the *Music & More CD*. Lead children to act out the suggested actions as you tell the story.

(Optional: Instead of playing sound effects, provide items kids can use to make sound effects: wooden blocks, kazoos, cellophane, thin metal baking sheets, etc.)

Law of Love

Exodus 19:1—20:21; 24:12; 25:10-22

A Message from God

Three months after leaving Egypt, the Israelites came to a BIG mountain called Mount Sinai. They set up their camp, facing the huge, jagged mountain.

  Moses climbed the rocky mountain to meet with God. **Show walking stick. Walk fingers upward.** God told Moses, "I have a message for you to give to My people. Tell them that if they will listen to what I say and keep My laws, then out of all the people in the world, THEY will be My own special treasure."

  Moses listened carefully. Then he hurried back down the mountain to where the Israelites had camped. **Walk fingers downward.** Moses called together the people and told them what God had said. They were glad—and they shouted together, "We will do everything God says!" Moses took off up the mountain again to tell God what the people had said. **Walk fingers upward.**

  God said to Moses, "Tell everyone to get ready. Something AMAZING is going to happen—I am going to come near the mountain in a thick cloud. The people will be able to HEAR My voice. Then they'll believe you when you tell them things I say to you."

God gave Moses more instructions for the people. Moses listened carefully and then hurried back down the mountain to tell the people what God had said. **Walk fingers downward.**

Preparing for the Visit

Moses told the people, "Here's what God said. The day after tomorrow God is going to come near to us. We must get ready! First, we must make ourselves clean—including all of our clothes." **Show soap, bowl and washcloth. Pretend to wash.**

Show caution tape. Then, we must set up a boundary around the mountain," Moses said. "The Lord said that NO one is to go up on the mountain—or even touch the boundary. You may only go NEAR the boundary when you hear a long, loud blast from the Lord's trumpet." The boundary around the mountain showed that the mountain was a holy, special place because GOD would be there!

So the whole camp got busy washing themselves and their clothes. They must have been excited to know that God was coming near them—He must have something VERY important to tell them!

Play "Thunder" sound effect from CD. Show lightning bolt cutout. Finally, the important day arrived with loud claps of thunder, flashes of lightning, a thick cloud covering the mountain and a LOUD trumpet blast. **Play "Trumpet" sound effect** from CD. Wow! **Shudder.** All of the Israelite people shuddered in fear and amazement.

Show Session 5 Bible Story Poster A. Moses led the people out of the camp to meet God. They stood near the boundary by the base of the mountain, waiting to hear God's important message.

Mount Sinai was covered with smoke. The whole mountain shook with earthquakes. **Play "Earthquake" sound effect from CD.** The trumpet blasts grew louder and LOUDER. **Play "Trumpet" sound effect from CD. Shudder and cover ears.**

God's Commandments

All the people were TERRIFIED. Then God spoke to His people and gave them His instructions for living life the best way.

Show four fingers. The first four commands told how God's people were to worship and show respect for Him. **Count on a finger for each commandment.** The people were to worship ONLY God, and not ANYONE else! God also said the people were not to make or worship any statues, as the people around them did. The Israelites were not to misuse His name in any way. They were to rest on the seventh day of the week and not work, as a way to honor God.

Show six fingers. God gave SIX more commands—about how people should treat each other. **Count on a finger for each commandment.** People were to respect their parents. There was to be NO killing other people. Husbands and wives were to keep their wedding promises. The people should NEVER steal things. They were not to tell lies about each other. The people were to be happy with what they had and NOT want other people's things for themselves.

The people were VERY afraid after hearing God's voice. They said to Moses, "YOU speak to us! We'll listen. But if God speaks to us, we'll DIE!"

"Don't be afraid," Moses told them. "God has shown you some of His mighty power so you will REMEMBER how strong He is. He wants you to obey His good commands!"

Walk fingers upward. Moses turned and hiked once more up the smoke-covered mountain. He listened to more of God's instructions for the Israelites.

God even wrote His commands on slabs of stone for Moses to give to the Israelites. And God then told Moses exactly how to make a beautiful box that would hold these Ten Commandments written on stone. This chest was going to be filled with things that reminded everyone of God's instructions and His promises to them!

Skit Option

Teachers, youth helpers or other volunteers perform "Fire on the Mountain!" on pages 47-48.

Conclusion

God's commands were SO important that God wanted His people to pay attention! That's why He sent earthquakes and thunder and lightning! He spoke His commands to the people Himself—they actually heard His voice from the mountain! God gave these commands because He wants everyone to know the best way to live.

Show Session 5 Bible Story Poster B. God knew that none of us can obey His commands perfectly. But Jesus did! When Jesus lived on Earth, He obeyed God perfectly. He never broke ONE of God's laws. This was something no one else ever did before or since! Because Jesus NEVER sinned, He was the only one who could take the punishment for our sin. He did this because He loves us!

Jesus also gave us a command. He said it was His NEW command. His command tells us the best way to live! In John 13:34 Jesus said, "A new command I give you: Love one another. As I have loved you, so you must love one another." Wow! Jesus wants us to love others as much as HE loves US! That is a LOT of love. But if we ask Him, Jesus will help us love people that much!

This week at VBS, we've talked about Ultimate Points, things God gives us as members of His family. We can be a part of God's Ultimate Plan. We can experience His Ultimate Power. We can be saved through Jesus' Ultimate Rescue. We can have Ultimate Trust in Jesus. And today we're talking about Ultimate Love—how Jesus tells us to love others and then helps us to DO that!

 The first step to loving God and loving others is to become a member of God's family. (Invite children interested in knowing more about becoming members of God's family to talk with you or another teacher after class. See "Leading a Child to Christ" on the inside back cover.)

Prayer

One way we can show love for others is to pray for them. Invite volunteers to name people for whom they would like to pray. Lead children in prayer, inviting children to say those names to complete the following sentence: **Thank You, Jesus, for loving us. Help us show Your love to . . ."** Close, thanking Jesus that He helps us show His love to others.

APPLY THE STORY
(10–15 minutes)

Bible Story Review

To review the Bible story, lead children to complete the "Color Words!" activity in *Head 'Em Out!* As children work, ask the questions below to guide conversation.

- ★ **Why did God give the Ten Commandments?** (To help God's people know the best way to live. So that His people would know how to show love to Him and to others.)

- ★ **What commands tell how to show love to and worship God?** (Worship only God. Don't make idols or statues to pray to. Respect God's name. Rest on the seventh day of the week to honor God.)

- ★ **Which of the commands tell us ways to love others?** (Respect parents. Don't kill. Husbands and wives keep their wedding promises. Don't steal. Don't tell lies. Don't want other people's things; be happy with what you have.)

- ★ **What are some ways kids your age can obey these commands? What are ways kids might disobey them?**

These commands gave God's people some basic rules to follow. But Jesus gave us a new rule: Love others in God's family. Ultimate Love is obeying Jesus' command and following Jesus' example by showing love to others. And we can ask Jesus to help us love others like that! Then we will be obeying His new command and living in the very best way!

Active Review

Children stand in a circle and toss or roll ball across the circle. Whenever ball leaves the circle, last player to touch it answers, or chooses a volunteer to answer, one of the questions on the previous page. Repeat as time allows.

Life Application

Read John 13:34 aloud with children from Bible or *Head 'Em Out!* **What is another way to say Jesus' new command?** (Love each other like Jesus loves us.) **What are some ways kids your age can show Jesus' love to others?** (Say kind words. Listen well. Pray for others. Help them when they need help.) **When we join God's family, we want to follow Jesus. We want to act like Him. So we ask Him to help us love others. It is a way to follow Him, or act the way He acts!**

Have children complete the "Loving Like Jesus Loves!" activity in *Head 'Em Out!* Ask questions such as:

★ **What are some ways to show you love Jesus?** (Obey Him. Read His Word. Give thanks to Him. Sing to Him.)

★ **What is your favorite way to show you love Jesus?** Accept all answers.

★ **What is a way you could show Jesus' love to other people?** (Listen to others. Be kind. Share.)

★ **Which of those ways could you do at home? At school? At the park?**

Ultimate Love means we show love to others because Jesus has shown us amazing love. If we are part of God's family, then we can ask Jesus to help us show His love to others. That's when we act like He acts. He will help us learn to follow Him and love God and others!

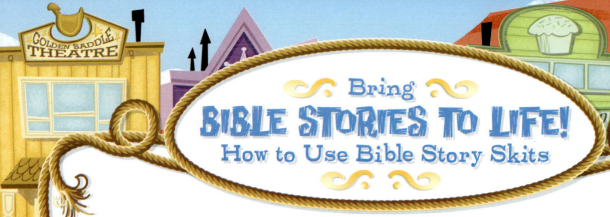

Bring Bible Stories to Life!
How to Use Bible Story Skits

Drama activities are valuable learning opportunities. What's most important is the process experienced by group members, not the quality of the final performance. Bible stories come alive when acted out! In addition:

- Acting out a situation will push children to think about the application of Bible truth to a real-life circumstance.
- Dramatic activities provide a unique opportunity to briefly step into other people's shoes and experience some of their attitudes and feelings.

Ways to Use Bible Story Skits in Your VBS

- Instead of telling the story as written in *Saddle Up! Bible Stories,* ask preteen kids to perform the skits for their own classes or for children in younger grades. These skits take approximately three to five minutes to perform.
- Ask older children and/or youth helpers to present the Bible story skits as a review during a 10-day VBS (see suggested schedule in Folder C of the *Director's Planning Guide CD-ROM*).
- Present one or more skits as part of your Closing Program.

Getting Ready

After you've chosen and reproduced copies of the skit for the participants, here are some tips for preparing to present the skit:

- Read the Scripture passage. Familiarize yourself with the corresponding Bible story as presented in any age-level *Saddle Up! Bible Stories.*
- Read the entire skit, noting any vocabulary or pronunciation help you will need to give your performers.
- Adapt the script if needed by reducing or increasing the number of characters, by adding a scene, etc.

Practical Tips

One of the nicest things about these Bible-story skits is that they are easy to prepare. Skits are not big Broadway-type productions. They can be informal and spontaneous. They can be primped and polished to the hilt when the mood strikes. A lot or a little—it all depends on how you want to do it. Here are the basics:

- Good acting is a plus, but it's not essential in order to have a positive experience. What is essential is that the lines are heard by the audience. The performers need to speak slowly and clearly—with their voices directed to the audience.
- If advance preparation and memorization isn't possible, you may choose to have actors read the scripts as they act them out. Provide several highlighter pens for performers to mark their parts.
- Always have extra copies of the script on hand.
- Practicing the skits ahead of time will be most important for younger groups and children for whom English is a second language.
- Though not necessary, Bible-times costumes add a nice touch for Bible-times characters.
- Optional: Print the setting of each scene to make signs. Have a volunteer hold up signs to announce the change of scene.

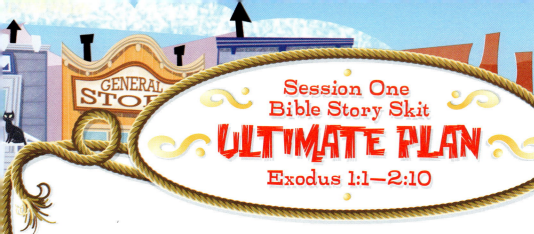

Session One
Bible Story Skit
ULTIMATE PLAN
Exodus 1:1—2:10

Characters

Narrator

Father, an Israelite father

Mother, an Israelite mother

Miriam, their daughter

Princess, Pharaoh's daughter

Maid 1 and Maid 2, Princess' maids

Characters may pantomime props.

Script

Scene 1: Home of Moses' family

Narrator: Our story begins in ancient Egypt, near the banks of the Nile River. The Egyptian Pharaoh is worried that the Israelites he keeps as slaves will one day rise up and take over. So he has issued a terrible order: Kill all the Israelite baby boys! But one brave family has kept their infant son hidden for three months.

(**Father** paces; **Mother** calmly weaves a basket.)

Father: This can't go on much longer. I can't take the stress. Will the baby cry? Will Pharaoh's soldiers hear him? Will they take him away? Something must be done!

Mother: I agree. That's why I'm weaving this basket.

Father: How can a basket keep the baby safe?

Mother: A basket can't keep him safe, but God can. Look, we can't keep the baby quiet forever. Sooner or later, Pharaoh's men WILL hear him.

Father: True . . . True . . .

Mother: But what if they DON'T find a baby here? What if instead of trusting in our ability to hide the baby, we trust God? Here's my plan: I weave a basket. I cover it with tar to make it waterproof. Then I put the baby inside and take the basket to the Nile River.

Father: So the basket becomes a boat! Where do you plan for it to go?

Mother: That's up to God. We simply trust that God has a PLAN for the baby.

Father: The river can be dangerous! I've seen crocodiles on the river . . . And what about Pharaoh's men?

Mother: I'm sure we can trust God with our baby.

Father: (*Reluctantly.*) OK, I'm sure you're right, but I wish we could know what will happen to our son. (*Thinking.*)

Mother: So do I.

Father: I know! Our daughter Miriam can help you take the basket to the river. Then she will hide, see what happens and come home to tell us!

Mother: Yes! Then we'll know what happens to him.

39

This will be so difficult! We're going to have to pray and trust that God has a plan for our baby.

Scene 2: Nile River

Narrator: Later that day, Miriam hides in the reeds, anxiously waiting to see what will happen to her baby brother.

Miriam: (*Praying with eyes closed.*) Dear God, please keep my baby brother from drowning or being captured by Pharaoh's men or eaten by crocodiles! Amen. (*Opens eyes and sees* **Princess** *and* **Maids** *approaching.*) Oh, no! It's Pharaoh's daughter!

Princess: Oooooh! I can't wait for a nice bath in the Nile! The squishy mud, the cool water . . .

Maid 1: (*Whispering.*) The snapping crocodiles.

Maid 2: (*Whispering.*) The swirling currents.

Maid 1: (*Whispering.*) The biting insects.

Princess: What was that?

Maids: (*Together.*) Nothing, your highness!

Miriam: (*To herself.*) Maybe she won't see the basket!

Princess: (*Pointing off stage right.*) Is that a basket floating behind those reeds? Bring it here!

Maid 2: (*Crosses stage right, peering offstage.*) It's just a soggy old basket. Someone as wealthy and powerful as you must have THOUSANDS of baskets nicer than that one!

Miriam: (*To herself.*) Okay, she's SEEN the basket. But maybe she won't want it!

Princess: I said, "Bring it here!"

Miriam: (*To herself.*) Okay, so she WANTS the basket. But maybe she won't open it? Maybe the baby won't cry?

(**Maid 1** *picks up basket and brings it to the* **Princess**.)

Princess: (*Opening basket.*) Look! It's a baby! And he's crying! (**Miriam** *shakes her head sadly.*)

Maid 1: (*Sticking fingers in ears.*) He sure has a good set of lungs on him!

Princess: He's very cute. Poor little guy must be hungry. Don't cry, little one. (*To* **Maids**.) How can we feed him?

Miriam: (*Stepping out of the reeds, speaking nervously.*) Um, your highness? Um . . . I could . . . if you wanted—

Princess: Speak up, girl! What is it?

Miriam: Would you like me to find an Israelite woman to nurse the baby for you?

Princess: Yes, go!

Narrator: A short time later, Miriam returns with her mother.

Miriam: This lady says she'd be happy to help you with the baby!

Princess: (*Handing baby to* **Mother**.) Take this baby and nurse him for me, and I will pay you.

Mother: Yes, your highness! I will!

(**Miriam** *and* **Mother** *walk away, carrying the baby and the basket.*)

Miriam: Mother, that was the BEST plan!

Mother: Trusting God is ALWAYS the best plan, Miriam.

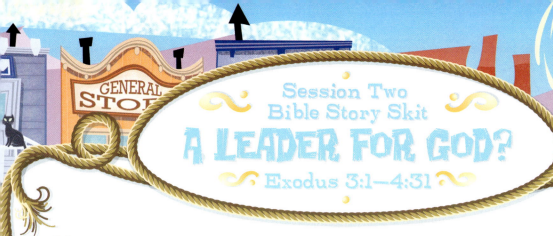

Session Two Bible Story Skit
A LEADER FOR GOD?
Exodus 3:1—4:31

Characters

Moses, God's newly appointed leader of the Hebrews

Aaron, Moses' brother

Characters may pantomime props.

Script

Scene: The mountain of Horeb

Aaron: Moses! Moses!

Moses: Aaron, is that you?

Aaron: No, it's my twin brother.

Moses: Aaron, you don't have a twin. I'm the only brother you've got.

Aaron: It was a joke! Look, I got a message to meet you here.

Moses: Yes, Aaron. I've seen God! And talked with Him!

Aaron: You SAW God and you're still alive to tell about it? R-i-i-ght.

Moses: Well, actually, what I saw was a burning bush.

Aaron: You think God is a burning bush? R-i-i-ght.

Moses: God isn't a burning bush, Aaron, that's just the way He got my attention!

Aaron: R-i-i-ght. So you talked to this burning bush . . .

Moses: Yes, and God told me . . .

Aaron: Hold it! This burning bush talked?

Moses: It wasn't really a burning bush. It was God.

Aaron: How do you know?

Moses: Because, well, the bush didn't burn up, and besides, He said He was.

Aaron: And you believed a talking bush? R-i-i-ght.

Moses: He said He was the God of our father and of Abraham and of Jacob. He's the God who promised to always be with us.

Aaron: Did you ask Him His name?

Moses: He said it was "I AM WHO I AM."

Aaron: (*Gulps.*) What did I AM WHO I AM want you to do?

Moses: He wants ME to go to Pharaoh and demand that he let the Hebrew slaves go free!

Aaron: YOU? Who's going to believe YOU?

Moses: Well, I asked Him the same question.

Aaron: You QUESTIONED God and lived? R-i-i-ght. What did He say?

Moses: He showed me three awesome ways to prove what I say is from God.

Aaron: Like what?

Moses: If I throw this stick on the ground, it becomes a snake.

Aaron: A SNAKE? R-i-i-ght.

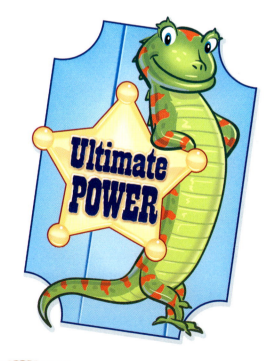

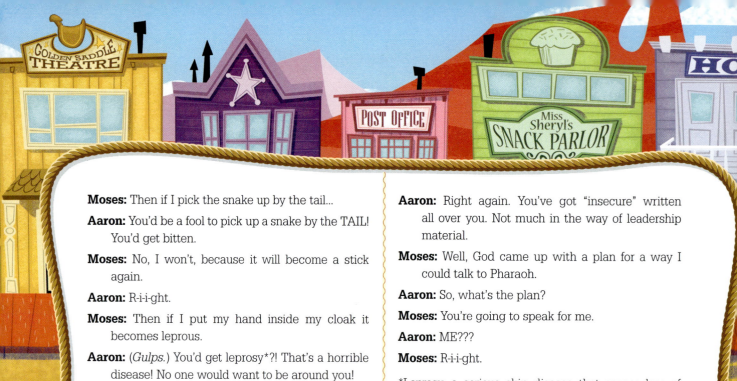

Moses: Then if I pick the snake up by the tail...

Aaron: You'd be a fool to pick up a snake by the TAIL! You'd get bitten.

Moses: No, I won't, because it will become a stick again.

Aaron: R-i-i-ght.

Moses: Then if I put my hand inside my cloak it becomes leprous.

Aaron: (*Gulps.*) You'd get leprosy*?! That's a horrible disease! No one would want to be around you!

Moses: Aaron! Calm down! When I put my hand back inside my cloak, it becomes healthy again.

Aaron: Well, I guess that WOULD be pretty impressive.

Moses: And He said if people still don't believe me, I am to go to the Nile to get water in a jug and then pour the water on the ground and it'll turn into blood!

Aaron: Blood! Yuck!

Moses: Don't you see? It will prove to those Egyptians that our God is the only God and that their god of the Nile is just a fake.

Aaron: I think it'll take more than a few miracles to get Pharaoh to give up all his slaves. But what happens next?

Moses: I lead the people out of Egypt.

Aaron: You? A leader? R-i-i-ght. YOU'VE been hiding out in the desert for 40 years!

Moses: I know. I tried to tell God I wasn't much of a leader, but He insisted!

Aaron: You ARGUED with God and lived? R-i-i-ght.

Moses: I just pointed out I wasn't much of a speaker.

Aaron: You've got that right! You meet a stranger and you get so nervous you forget your name.

Moses: And I pointed out that I'm sort of a nobody, so who'd listen to me?

Aaron: Right again. You've got "insecure" written all over you. Not much in the way of leadership material.

Moses: Well, God came up with a plan for a way I could talk to Pharaoh.

Aaron: So, what's the plan?

Moses: You're going to speak for me.

Aaron: ME???

Moses: R-i-i-ght.

*Leprosy—a serious skin disease that causes loss of feeling and many deformities.

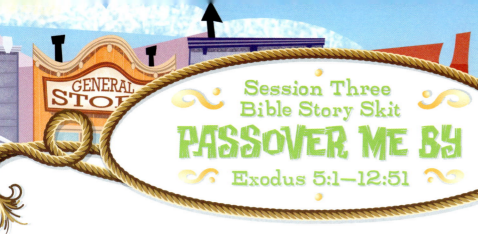

Session Three
Bible Story Skit
PASSOVER ME BY
Exodus 5:1–12:51

Characters

Pharaoh, king of Egypt

Advisor, Pharaoh's right-hand man

Characters may pantomime props.

Script

Scene: Pharaoh's palace in Egypt

Pharaoh: Goodness, but it's dark. Not as dark as a few days ago, but dark. I wish I could get some sleep. Advisor!

Advisor: (*Enters, rubbing sleep from his eyes.*) Yes, my king.

Pharaoh: Were you asleep?

Advisor: (*Stops rubbing eyes suddenly.*) Me? Asleep while Pharaoh is awake? Oh, no. Never, never, never.

Pharaoh: Then why were you rubbing your eyes?

Advisor: (*Stammering sleepily.*) Why? Umm, why was I rubbing my eyes? Something. I was rubbing. Why? Aha! I was rubbing my eyes because something was in my eye. Dust? A louse? That's it. I had a speck of louse in my eye.

Pharaoh: Just so you weren't asleep. I can't sleep.

Advisor: Perhaps you should count sheep, O King.

Pharaoh: Don't need to. You know my plan for getting to sleep.

Advisor: (*Horrified.*) Not . . .

Pharaoh: Yes. The historical method. Read to me from the history book.

(**Advisor** *stumbles to shelf or table and brings out large book.*)

Advisor: Is there any special part Pharaoh would care to hear?

Pharaoh: Anywhere is fine.

Advisor: (*Opens book and begins reading.*) . . . and it came to pass that Joseph . . .

Pharaoh: Joseph! Again with this Joseph! Who is Joseph?

Advisor: I don't know.

Pharaoh: Well, find out.

(**Advisor** *flips backward through book, mumbling as though reading quickly.*)

Pharaoh: So who is Joseph? Moses talks about him. The history books tell of him.

Advisor: Ah, I have it. (*Reads.*) ". . . and the Israelite prisoner, Joseph, was elevated in rank and set in charge of collecting twenty percent of all the food produced in Egypt." He seems to have been a tax collector, Sire.

43

Pharaoh: All this fuss over a tax collector? Amazing.

Advisor: (*Consulting book.*) And he apparently saved Egypt from great famine.

Pharaoh: Oh. A hero. How long ago did this happen?

Advisor: About four hundred years ago, Sire.

Pharaoh: Oh. Ancient history. Nothing for me to worry about, then.

Advisor: No, your highness.

Pharaoh: (*Stands.*) Reading isn't helping. Maybe a midnight snack. What have we got?

Advisor: Frog legs, Sire.

Pharaoh: STILL?

Advisor: They were plentiful this year, Your Majesty.

Pharaoh: Well, I'm tired of them.

Advisor: As are we all.

Pharaoh: (*Sits.*) As long as I can't sleep, I might as well get some work done.

Advisor: (*Starts to leave.*) I'll leave you to it, then.

Pharaoh: No. Stay. I need advice. (*Stares at* **Advisor**.) Your face . . .

Advisor: (*Confused.*) You need advice about my face, my lord?

Pharaoh: No! What's that hideous thing on your face?

Advisor: (*Touches cheek.*) A boil, Your Highness. Leftover from Plague Number Six.

Pharaoh: Oh. Well, do something about it.

Advisor: Maybe sleep can remove boils, O Pharaoh. I shall attend to it immediately. (*Turns to go.*)

Pharaoh: TOMORROW.

Advisor: (*Aside.*) I was afraid you'd say that.

Pharaoh: What about this latest threat from Moses?

Advisor: Has there been another? I haven't seen him since the great darkness. I wouldn't worry about what Moses and his people are up to.

Pharaoh: You haven't noticed the Israelites are spreading BLOOD all over their door posts?

Advisor: Just so they're not shedding blood in Egyptian houses, there's nothing to worry about.

Pharaoh: Then you think I'm doing the right thing, keeping the Israelites in Egypt?

Advisor: But of course, Sire. Where else will you find a slave labor force of six hundred thousand men? You have building projects to complete! You need the manpower!

Pharaoh: True. But some Egyptians are taking Moses' latest threat seriously.

Advisor: Such utter nonsense. NO god can find the firstborn of every family in Egypt. And not only people, but animals. Pharaoh, not even the SUN can do this. There's nothing to worry about.

Pharaoh: Well, I don't like all that blood. Makes the country look messy.

Advisor: Then teach the Israelites a lesson. Tomorrow, make them clean up all the blood AND make their full quota of bricks. Lean on them. Show them who's in charge.

Pharaoh: Hmm. That could work. Put a stop to all this trouble Moses has been causing.

(*Loud screams and crying from offstage.*)

Pharaoh: What happened? Go find out!

(**Advisor** *exits; crying continues.* **Advisor** *enters looking worried.*)

Pharaoh: Well, what is it?

Advisor: Um . . . Well, uh . . . Nothing too serious. Just a little accident.

Pharaoh: There seems to be a lot of commotion for a little accident. Who's been hurt?

Advisor: Ahem. Well. (*Counts on fingers.*) The heir to the throne seems to have died. And the chambermaid's firstborn. And that of the queen's attendants. And the oldest of the palace cat's litter. The oldest of the footman, the butcher, the baker, the candlestick maker, the . . .

(**Pharaoh** *runs offstage, upset.*)

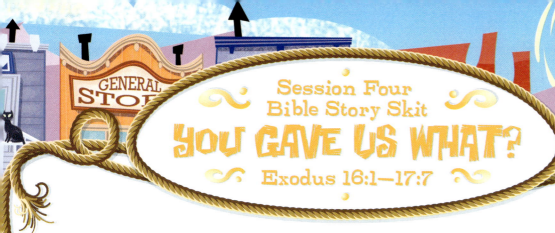

Session Four Bible Story Skit
YOU GAVE US WHAT?
Exodus 16:1—17:7

Characters

Narrator
Kid 1, Kid 2, Israelite kids
Moses, Israelite leader
Aaron, Moses' brother and Israelite leader
Characters may pantomime props.

Script

Scene 1: Afternoon

Narrator: Our friends the Israelites have been out in the desert for about a month now . . . and most of their food supplies are used up. They do not see any water around, either. If you know anything about the Israelites, they had one great talent—COMPLAINING. And guess what they were doing again? (*Pauses for audience to respond.*) That's right! Com-PLAIN-ing!

(**Kid 1** and **Kid 2** enter.)

Kid 1: I'm so HUNGRY!

Kid 2: Why are you telling me? I'm hungry, too!

Kid 1: Well, it's not like I can complain to my parents. They're doing enough complaining of their own.

Kid 2: You're telling me? You can hear the grownups from here! (*Puts hand to ear, listening.*) Now they're asking Moses, "Why did you bring us out here to STARVE?"

Kid 1: I just hope Moses does something about it soon!

(**Kid 1** and **Kid 2** exit.)

Narrator: Meanwhile, God had already heard the complaining. He already was sending His help! So Moses and Aaron called the people together.

(**Aaron** and **Moses** enter, addressing audience as if they are the Israelites.)

Moses: (*Cupping hands around mouth, gestures.*) Come here, everyone! Could we have quiet, please? God has heard your complaining. After all, when you complain, you are not complaining about US—you're complaining about HIM!

Aaron: God wants you to know that He's heard everything you've said. And this is what He told Moses about it: "At sunset, you will eat meat. In the morning you will be filled with bread. Then you will know that I am the Lord your God."

Moses: So quiet down, will you? Get to your tents. Wait to see what God will do! (*Makes shooing gestures.*) Go! GO!

Scene 2: Evening

(**Kid 1** and **Kid 2** enter. **Kid 1** pats his stomach.)

Kid 1: Wow! Am I ever full!

Kid 2: Isn't that just the craziest thing? I never thought I would be grabbing quail right out of the air! They're small, but tasty!

Kid 1: God did a GREAT job with the meat part! (*Pats

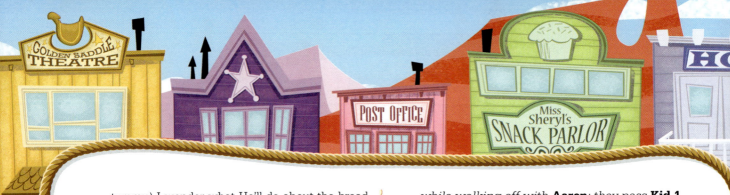

tummy.) I wonder what He'll do about the bread part of His promise?

Kid 2: Beats me. But since the quail were so good, I'm thinking the bread should be AWESOME!

Kid 1: Yeah! Well, I gotta go to bed. I'm so full I can hardly move! G'night!

Kid 2: G'night!

(**Kid 1** and **Kid 2** wave to each other as they walk off in opposite directions.)

Scene 3: Morning

(**Aaron** and **Moses** enter, addressing audience as if they are the Israelites. **Moses** carries a basket.)

Aaron: Well, I guess you've all seen it by now . . .

Moses: But have you TASTED it? (Reaches into basket, puts something in his mouth.) Umm . . . UMM! Yummm!! It's GREAAAT!! (**Moses** continues to eat while **Aaron** talks.)

Aaron: (Appears to take a question from the audience.) You want to know what it is? Well, truth is, we don't know! So how about we call it "manna"? That means, "What is it?" (Looks around for approval, claps his hands.) Good. Done. Next?

Moses: So listen, all of you. Gather all you want today. God says it will be there on the ground tomorrow, too. But on the day before the Sabbath, gather TWICE as much. That way, you can rest on the Sabbath and obey God.

Aaron: You can leave it overnight, but only on the night before the Sabbath. Otherwise, it'll get nasty and be full of worms. Trust me, you don't want to eat that! You'll call it "Yucca" instead of "Manna"! (Chuckles at his own joke.)

(**Moses** and **Aaron** exit; **Moses** continues to eat while walking off with **Aaron**; they pass **Kid 1** and **Kid 2** coming onstage and all greet each other adlib as they pass.)

Kid 1: (Bends down, picks up something.) What IS this? It looks like . . . like nothing I've ever seen before! (Puts it in his mouth, picks up more and puts it in his mouth.)

Kid 2: (Looks up at the sky.) God, you gave us THIS? It's really good! It's not like anything I've ever eaten! But it doesn't have a name.

Kid 1: (Mumbles as if mouth is full.) "Manna." Aaron said to call it "manna."

Kid 2: What? BaNANA?

Kid 2: (Wipes mouth.) No, no—MANNA. Like, "What is it?"

Kid 1: Think we can make ba-MANNA bread out of this?

Kid 2: Or maybe . . . MANNA-cotti? (**Kid 1** and **Kid 2** laugh.)

Kid 2: (**Kid 1** and **Kid 2** look up, shout in unison.) Whatever it is, Thank You, God!

(**Kid 1** and **Kid 2** exit.)

Session Five Bible Story Skit
FIRE ON THE MOUNTAIN!
Exodus 19:1—20:21; 24:12; 25:10-22

Characters

Narrator
Kid 1, Kid 2, Israelite kids
Moses, Israelite leader
Miriam, Moses' sister
Characters may pantomime props.

Script

Scene 1: Camped at Sinai

Narrator: The Israelites have been traveling for EXACTLY three months. Three months to the day since they left Egypt, they have now stopped their travels to camp in front of Mount Sinai. And where is Moses, their leader? He's currently somewhere up on that mountain, talking with God!

(**Kid 1** and **Kid 2** enter, talking as they walk.)

Kid 1: Did you hear what Moses said when he came down the mountain yesterday? He keeps talking with God! It's amazing!

Kid 2: Yeah, I heard that God HIMSELF is going to come to the top of this mountain in a thick cloud and talk so we can hear Him!

Kid 1: My mom is going crazy washing all our clothes! That's what Moses said to do. And did you hear all of the grownups? They were shouting, "We will do EVERYTHING the Lord has said!"

Kid 2: Yeah, I sure hope they mean it. They usually complain when God tells them to do something!

(**Kid 1** and **Kid 2** continue to walk and are intercepted by **Miriam**.)

Miriam: (Several stones in her hand, gestures wildly.) Stop right there, you two! You're right at the boundary of the mountain! Don't touch! Do NOT touch! You could DIE!

Kid 1: Whoa! Sounds like a good reason to stop! But what are YOU doing out here, Miss Miriam? Aren't you kind of in the way of danger, too?

Miriam: I'm laying out stones so that people can tell where the boundary is! (Points to imaginary line of stones.) See? Knowing where the boundary is will keep people safe. They'll know where to stop, so they don't accidentally touch the mountain.

Kid 2: Shoot, Miss Miriam. (Looks around.) It's a BIG mountain. We'll help you! (To **Kid 1**.) There are plenty of stones around here! Let's help Miss Miriam lay 'em down.

Miriam: When God comes to the mountain, we'll hear a trumpet. That will be our signal that it's safe to come near. But until then, making a boundary can help people stay safe!

(All exit, pretending to pick up and lay down stones in a line as they go.)

47

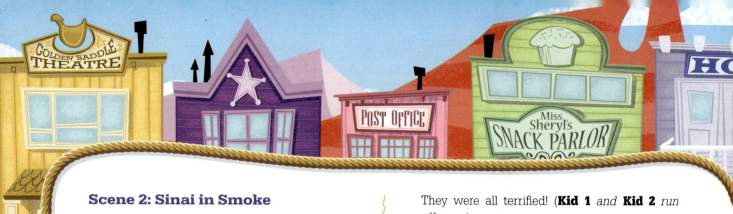

Scene 2: Sinai in Smoke

Narrator: Today is the big day. The sun has come up and now God has come down to meet Moses and the Israelites. The top of the mountain is covered in a rolling, dark, thick cloud. Lightning bolts are shooting in every direction and loud thunder rumbles out waves of sound. Everything is trembling with the tremendous power of God! On top of that, thick smoke is rising all around, because God has come down in fire! Wow!

(**Moses** *enters, addresses audience as if they are the Israelites.*)

Moses: Israelites! Today is the day! You all have been made ready to meet God. You will hear things that no one has ever heard before. Look! God Himself has come down in fire! And I know you all feel the earth shaking! So don't forget! The mountain is HOLY. God is there. Do NOT touch the mountain! (*Points.*) Notice the boundary! Don't even go near it until you hear the sound of a trumpet. I'm going now. (**Moses** *turns to leave, then turns back to the audience, pointing.*) Don't forget! The boundary is there to protect you! (*Exits.*)

(**Kid 1** *and* **Kid 2** *enter opposite* **Moses**, *craning their necks, looking upward as they walk.*)

Kid 1: Wow. Wow! WOW!!!! This is big. This is AMAZING. This is . . .

Kid 2: (*Interrupts.*) GOD! God is up there! Hear that? That thunder is so HUGE! I bet that's God talking to Moses!

Kid 1: Let's get as close as we can. Race ya to the boundary!

Kid 2: OK, but I'm stopping there. Like Miss Miriam said, the boundary is here to keep us safe. And it looks to me like there is plenty of reason today to want to stay safe!

Kid 1: Yeah, that's what the grownups were saying, too. They stayed way back from the boundary. They were all terrified! (**Kid 1** *and* **Kid 2** *run offstage.*)

Narrator: And there, on the mountain where fire and smoke, clouds and lightning, thunder and earthquakes, all showed that God was present, Moses took Aaron and received God's commandments for His people to follow! These commands helped Israel honor God and honor each other. He promised to bless them as they obeyed His law. (*Gestures at the line of imaginary stones onstage.*) The commands God gave are like the boundary around the mountain. His laws are boundaries that keep us safe by telling us how to honor God and honor other people by not hurting them. God's laws are good. Because we human beings need God and need each other, obeying God's law helps us live in peace and love with Him and with everyone else!

The only thing is, even when we TRY to obey the law, we can't ever do it perfectly. We need Jesus. He came to take the punishment for our sin, so that as part of God's family, we can have Jesus' help to follow Him and obey His new law to love each other!